FROM THE
HEART
OF
GOD

Nine Strategies To Revolutionise Your Bible Reading

BY PASCAL SIME

Copyright © Pascal Sime 2023.

All rights reserved.

ISBN: 9798374813456

Independently published 2023.

Cover designed by TK Palad.

Edited By Janet de Vigne.

No part of this publication may be reproduced, stored in any retrieval system, or transmitted in any form of by any means, without the prior written permission of the publisher, nor be otherwise circulated in any form of binding or cover other than that in which it is published and without a similar condition being imposed on the subsequent purchaser.

The right of Pascal Sime to be identified as the author of the Work has been asserted by him in accordance with the Copyright, Designs and Patents Act 1988.

Scripture quotations [marked NIV] taken from the Holy Bible, New International Version Anglicised Copyright © 1979, 1984, 2011 Biblica. Used by permission of Hodder & Stoughton Ltd, an Hachette UK company. All rights reserved. 'NIV' is a registered trademark of Biblica UK trademark number 1448790.

Scripture quotations taken from the (NASB®) New American Standard Bible®, Copyright © 1960, 1971, 1977, 1995, 2020 by The Lockman Foundation. Used by permission. All rights reserved. lockman.org

Scripture quotations marked (NLT) are taken from the *Holy Bible*, New Living Translation, copyright ©1996, 2004, 2015 by Tyndale House Foundation. Used by permission of Tyndale House Publishers, Carol Stream, Illinois 60188. All rights reserved.

Scripture quotations are from the ESV® Bible (The Holy Bible, English Standard Version®), copyright © 2001 by Crossway, a publishing ministry of Good News Publishers. Used by permission. All rights reserved. The ESV text may not be quoted in any publication made available to the public by a Creative Commons license. The ESV may not be translated in whole or in part into any other language.

Scripture quotations marked TPT are from The Passion Translation®. Copyright © 2017, 2018, 2020 by Passion & Fire Ministries, Inc. Used by permission. All rights reserved. ThePassionTranslation.com.

For inquiries email pascalsime@hotmail.co.uk

Version 1.0

Dedicated to the life of my Stepfather Ronnie

I'm thankful for the joy he brought my Mum

I was honoured to baptise him and I'll be honoured to meet him again

Contents

INTRODUCTION
Carrying the bull — 9

ONE
Spiritual intuition — 19

TWO
Revelation tactics — 35

THREE
Inner biblical interpretation & handling your doubts about God — 47

FOUR
Becoming the book author/original readers — 63

FIVE
Study your calling — 79

SIX
Emotional simulation — 99

SEVEN
Looking for the bigger picture — 113

EIGHT
Getting hidden revelation from 'boring' verses — 127

NINE
Viewing life through scripture — 151

Acknowledgements — 167

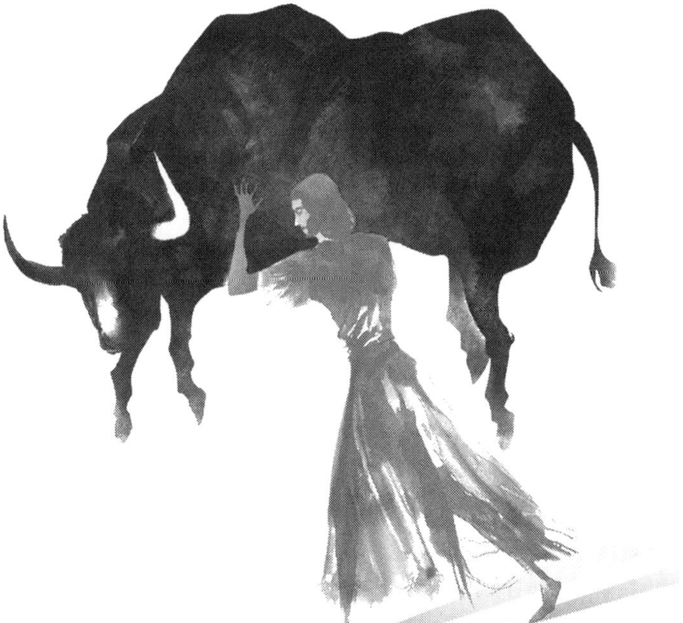

Introduction
Carrying the bull

There's an old story about a man who carried a calf around his shoulders from one village to another every day with the intention of getting stronger. Each day was the same routine. He would pick up the calf, wrap it around his shoulders, and begin his journey. The days turned to weeks, the weeks turned to months and the months turned to years.

As the calf was growing older it was also growing bigger and heavier. Meaning, the man carrying it was also progressively getting stronger slowly yet surely. Eventually, the calf grew up into a large bull, and alongside this, the man had become incredibly strong from carrying it each day. Every time he walked past anyone on his journey, they were so amazed cheering and clapping him on. He grew strong enough to be able to carry a bull around his shoulders from one village to the other, every single day.

The problem with this old story however, is that getting stronger does not work this way. Anyone that tries this strategy is never able to carry the bull. It might seem like a logical tactic, but getting stronger is not that simple because human bodies eventually stop getting stronger when the same repetitive stimulus is applied over and over again.

This same strategy applied to Bible reading has the same effect. If you read it every day, week, month and year the same way, you can expect to grow to a certain level, as a man carrying a calf would. But to use the same strategy and read it the same way over and over again will only get you so far in your journey.

If the man changed his strategy, do you think it's possible that he could carry the bull?

The world has changed

There have been countless people over the course of time who have had a desire to change the world. It seems to be a thing with humans. People who want to change things, to change themselves, to change attitudes, to change cultures and to improve things. You may have had this thought yourself at times.

A few years after I became a Christian, I realised that the world does not need to be changed in the way many people think, because the solution that brings about change has already come, 2000 years ago.

I realised that while people are trying to improve their lives and trying to fix their problems by coming up with new things, the solution had already happened long before they were even born. And so all that needs to happen now is that people know about this change.

What's the difference between a person trying to change the world their way in comparison to realising that the world has already been changed? The difference is that they stop trying to come up with new solutions to problems and recognize that the solution has already come, and so the difference is in the approach. It is not so much about finding a solution, but rather exploring the solution we already have, that being, our Lord and Saviour Jesus Christ.

Vision of this book

In this book, I want to present you with nine ways by which you can get more life out of your Bible reading. Some of these things you may already know about, some may be new to you. Take any ideas you like, leave other ones alone, it's up to you. When we read books I think the things that are supposed to stick are the things that do, and if there's anything you don't remember, don't worry about it.

My vision for this book is founded entirely on 1 Samuel 13:14 and so everything I write about hangs off this verse.

'The Lord has sought out for Himself a man after His own heart' 1 Samuel 13:14 (NASB)

We have this scene with Samuel the prophet, who is an advisor to King Saul, the first king of Israel. King Saul made some pivotal mistakes and then Samuel rebukes him. God had taken the kingdom away from Saul and given it to a man that was searching for God's own heart. This was a young shepherd boy called David.

In this book, I will present you with nine ways that you can search for the Lords own heart when reading your Bible, so you are in a better position to see life *'From The Heart Of God'*.

The purpose of this book is to do one thing - help you move into God's own heart, to feel what He feels, that is if you are willing. We're going to do this by learning how to receive revelation from Him and using Ephesians 1:17 as the basis for that. This is where the apostle Paul wrote to the church in Ephesus to strengthen the believers.

"I keep asking that the God of our Lord Jesus Christ, the glorious Father, may give you the spirit of wisdom and revelation, so that you may know him better." Ephesians 1:17 (NIV)

Jesus said He came to give us life in all its abundance, we receive this abundance by the revelation of the Holy Spirit. I want to teach you how to better position yourself to receive revelations from God, for you to live with His life flowing through your veins. I'm not suggesting you don't already know how to do this, but in the following chapters, I may be able to open things up for you a little more.

In every chapter, I am going to explain to you how to use a particular strategy and why it's important. You will see that it always points to the objectives of positioning yourself inside God's perspective and gaining revelation of Him.

In **CHAPTER ONE** we explore reading the Bible by having an intuition or sensitivity of the Holy Spirit, and how this is to be done alongside every other strategy I speak of in this book.

In **CHAPTER TWO** we explore how to prepare yourself to get revelation in your Bible reading. I will describe general tactics you can use to set the right conditions to hear from God powerfully for the rest of your life.

In **CHAPTER THREE** we explore an essential way to interpret the Bible and how the Bible itself is the greatest commentary there is. This is an important step, to trust God more comprehensively throughout your life and to deal with any doubts you may have about Him and His word.

In **CHAPTER FOUR** we explore how to experience scripture from the perspective of other people, namely the book author and the original intended readers/receivers of the book. By doing this we can feel more from scripture and see details that are easy to miss otherwise.

In **CHAPTER FIVE** we explore the art of studying your calling in the Bible, and how learning to take Bible studies into your own hands is an important step to realise your dreams.

In **CHAPTER SIX** we explore emotional simulation. This is where you put yourself in the shoes of all the characters in the passage you're reading, to experience the full emotional spectrum.

In **CHAPTER SEVEN** we explore seeing the bigger picture in the Bible story you're reading and why this is significant for you today.

In **CHAPTER EIGHT** we explore how to draw life from any verse in the Bible, particularly the ones you might consider boring. Learn how to do this and you learn how to embrace all scripture.

And finally, in **CHAPTER NINE** we explore how to view your life through scripture and how this is a powerful way to take God with you into your day, not just in your Bible reading sessions.

I admit that the dilemma with a book like this is that you may not be ready or even interested in some or even all of the strategies. So to counter this as best as I can, I have kept this book shorter than it could have been and decided to give you a *'flash in the pan'* of each strategy. I present the idea, give a couple of examples, then move on, it is up to you what you do with it, if anything. I do hope you enjoy this book, but my primary hope is to help you get more out of the Bible. This is a book about the most important book ever written.

Truth awaits

The Bible has changed my life and continues to do so. My Bible is pretty beaten up, I just tape it when the cover breaks. This isn't the kind of book we throw away, that's rule number one by the way, never throw a Bible in the bin (unless it has become unreadable). If you must, put it in someone's letterbox, but never throw it away.

The Bible contains 66 books inside it. It was written by approximately 40 authors over approximately 1500 years. There are over 1000 chapters containing over 30 thousand verses. It talks about the beginning of the world, the end of life as we know it, and many things that happen in between. We read this book because it gives us life. This book more than any other teaches us how to live life to the full.

Years before I became a Christian I had an intuition that there was a universal truth that would somehow direct people to the best life they could live. If you come to accept that God is the author of all truth and that He has captured much of this truth in the Bible, there is a powerful realisation that follows that this is the most important book you could ever read.

The greatest stage of a believer's existence that we know about from scripture, is when we are with the Lord in heaven. But for now, while we are still alive in this fallen world, you get to (in part), experience this greatest stage by learning about and living for God today. The faster you do that now, by experiencing the Bible, the greater your experience of life will be today. So it's better to do it sooner than later. In Hebrews 4:12 it says.

"For the word of God is living and active and sharper than any two-edged sword, and piercing as far as the division of soul and spirit, of both joints and marrow, and able to judge the thoughts and intentions of the heart." Hebrews 4:12 (NASB)

Such a powerful verse, but sometimes it's helpful to simplify it a little. So I'll take out the middle section so it says this.

"For the word of God is living and active - and able to judge the thoughts and intentions of the heart"

What does that mean? Well there is something profoundly powerful about God's word, because it's truth, it's God's written source of truth, and so when we read it, it's able to judge the thoughts and intentions of our heart. It calls out the truth from within us, amongst all the thoughts in our heads. It's like I always believed, that the pursuit of truth would somehow take us to where we're supposed to go. The Bible guides and augments this journey for us.

Why do we even have the Bible?

The Bible itself gives us the answer in 2 Timothy 3:15. Where the apostle Paul says we have scripture to make us *wise to salvation*. That's why we have this, to help bring us to the point where we say yes to following Jesus. Why do we continue to read it after that point? It answers this in the next two verses.

"All Scripture is inspired by God and is useful to teach us what is true and to make us realize what is wrong in our lives. It corrects us when we are wrong and teaches us to do what is right. God uses it to prepare and equip his people to do every good work" 2 Timothy 3:16-17 (NLT)

So the Bible is there to make us wise to salvation and to teach us. Using these nine strategies is going to help you to read the Bible and receive life from it, drawing you closer to the heart of God. We sometimes refer to scripture as the living word, which means that it's alive and relevant in your life today.

When you learn any skill, the art of making it a part of your instincts or your nature, begins first by learning it and then the regular practice of it. And so I want to explore this with you and come to the last phase of learning a skill at the end of the book. God's search for a person after His own heart did not end when He found David.

Let's begin...

Chapter One
Spiritual intuition

"When the Spirit of truth comes, he will guide you into all the truth" John 16:13 (ESV)

"There were various strategies I learned to gain confidence with my sling. Using a figure of eight motion gave me better momentum than a circular one. Having one foot in front of the other gave me greater stability than having my feet parallel. When I first started, I used to spend several seconds building up speed with the sling before I released the stone, but eventually, I learned how to do it quickly because I wouldn't normally have time to prepare shots for long in the field.

But it wasn't until an old-looking shepherd came over when I was practising, and told me something I never considered before. He said there were two kinds of shepherds "shepherds that hit their targets using their head, and shepherds that hit their targets using their heart". He said no more than this and then walked off with a facial expression that I always remembered. It was the kind of smile that a father gives to their son, it was *as if he was telling me which of the two shepherds I was. I wanted to ask him more, but something told me that what he just said was the last step to mastering my sling.*

From that day on I started to sling stones differently, I felt freer after that. In a sense, I just let go of all my knowledge, and from that day on I slung stones with my heart. I rarely missed my targets after that.

Soon after this, I tried to find the old shepherd so I could thank him, but I found no trace or history of him. It was as if he vanished into thin air. Years later I realised that God brought him into my life for a bigger reason than I could see at that time. At the time I just wanted to protect my sheep with my sling, I didn't realise that I was preparing to protect men with it."

— King David sharing stories with his warriors (story re-imagined by the author)

The Bible...God's word...it can be read in many ways. Many strategic approaches can be learned to help you get more life from it. But these strategies become most powerful only when we let go of them. Only when we let go of them do they become natural, or even... spiritual.

Is the Bible to be read with our heads? Yes, yes it is. But even more than this, it is to be read with our hearts, to know God's heart.

I want to tell you about reading the Bible in partnership with the way God has designed us to understand things. I want to tell you about what I call... *spiritual intuition.*

We all have intuitions in life. They come into formation because a specific recollection of our past experience has been brought into the forefront of our memory from something.

When reading the Bible, do you ever have an awareness of intuitions in the innermost part of your mind? Feelings that run deeper than your thoughts. We all have intuitions and they come with little or no conscious effort; they are not as obvious as the more analytical thoughts in our minds. When reading the Bible, these intuitions can function as signposts to where God can take us.

Having awareness of your spiritual intuition when reading the Bible often means exploring what lies behind your thoughts, and an important Bible reading skill is having the ability to be able to identify these intuitions and flesh them out into personal revelation.

How do you identify an intuition?

While reading the Bible you may have an intuition that blends gently into your conscious mind. Intuitions can come as unassuming whispers into your spirit, not as clear and obvious as pronounced thoughts.

There are varying depths of intuitions. Some may be more obvious and require no contemplation to reel them into your consciousness. Some are further inside the depths of your thoughts and require deeper contemplation to bring them to clearer awareness. And further still, some may be too deep for you to reach today (even though you can sense them), but through your maturity and in walking with Christ, they will eventually rise.

Having an intuition requires little or no conscious effort - it is like automated spiritual promptings that require no processing power from your thinking. You don't need to try to have an intuition, it can simply happen from reading a verse. After this, you do what you can to have an awareness of it. I find that re-reading the same scripture several times over is a powerful way to do this.

Pausing to consider what you have read to have an awareness of any underlying thoughts helps us to dig further into the spirit. It takes time for your mind to catch up with what you're reading - stopping to consider and contemplate every few verses is a powerful way to become aware of an intuition.

When we read scripture with busy minds, it may be harder to identify an intuition among our many thoughts. Closing your eyes and resting your head on something can be a good physical position to consider and explore any intuition inspired by scripture. It requires such deep and concentrated thought that sometimes we need to physically get into a position that helps us to focus to *'pull'* the intuition out of our thoughts.

Having the ability to gently reel in these intuitions is a wonderful spiritual skill and shows us that Bible reading can be an amazing creative journey that can take us somewhere we don't expect, just as God's voice often does. I once heard someone say: 'you're never closer to God than when you're being creative' - a wonderful insight I hope to explore with you.

What do you do with an intuition if you have one?

While we become aware of our intuitions from contemplation, we explore them with meditation and then use our existing biblical knowledge to turn them into something - to bring biblical stability to them. The idea is that we turn our intuitions into revelation, a powerful and personal truth revealed. On their own, they might not go far and have an insignificant effect on us. Like signposts, they show us where to go, but they won't take us anywhere unless we move in their direction.

When you read the Bible like this you don't directly choose what your intuition will be, the same way you don't choose where the signposts go in the street. It's our life experience that is the source of our intuitions, and whether these are chosen experiences or ones we've had no say in, they become the bank of experiences that our spiritual intuition draws from while reading.

We can learn about life experiences in the life of Moses. He was born into, and grew up in, circumstances that developed an emotional concern for his people, the Israelites in his heart (Exodus 1 & 2). God didn't click his fingers and Moses suddenly cared for his people out of nowhere, no, his life experience produced this. When you look at what people were called to in the Bible, often the calling is a response to the most emotional or significant experiences that happened in their past.

Think of the most extreme emotions or experiences from your past. Have you noticed a link between these experiences and the things you've been called to, or could be called to?

We can see through this that our intuitions when reading scripture, which are links to our past, are also directly linked to our future, to our callings. Our intuitions can be spiritual bridges between our previous pains, prominent life experiences, broken dreams, traumas and so-called failures, all the way to God's glory (the bigger purpose of our spiritual intuitions).

Spiritual intuition

If you choose to spend time in God's word regularly, living by His word and living a Christian lifestyle, whatever that looks like in your culture, then you are investing into a kingdom-cultured box of intuitions that will come back to inform you about God's heart while reading scripture.

There can be a fear in Christians when reading the Bible like this (exploring our intuitions to see where they take us). Why? Because at some point you may have been told *'don't read into the scriptures'* or something to that effect. But the scriptures might inspire trails of thought that lead us to depths of insight that the biblical text does not seem to be addressing directly. I encourage you to enjoy your freedom in Christ, follow your intuitions and see where God takes you, as long as this process remains biblical and honouring to Him.

I should say though, that despite this attempt to keep things right, how can you ensure you won't manipulate scripture into saying something it is not? After all, in the book of Jeremiah, it says **"The heart is deceitful above all things, and desperately sick; who can understand it?" Jeremiah 17:9 (ESV)**

The heart is often used metaphorically to describe our emotions. God calls us to be obedient to Him, not to our emotions, despite their possible links to our callings. At times, I have had a revelation in scripture to then realise later that my 'revelation' was theologically false, and therefore not a Godly revelation at all. So it's a healthy move to discuss these things with other Christians to test out what you're thinking, and not build your beliefs from unstable platforms.

Our intuitions need a helping hand. It is an intuition after all and not a fully fleshed-out revelation yet. When you have an intuition that God is saying something to you in the scriptures, it may be wise to encourage this intuition by becoming more informed on its subject and avoiding building on non-truths.

Reading commentaries, watching videos, talking to your pastors and discussing things in Bible groups will test your revelation. From here you can enjoy and develop a more biblically founded and trusted intuitiveness. Learn how to notice your intuitions, encourage them through study and develop them into something. This all becomes a time of training on how to hear Him, your heart to His heart.

While we can follow our intuitions when reading the Bible, perhaps the authors of the Bible followed their intuitions while writing it. I have wondered whether the authors had any idea how brilliant their books were when they wrote them - if they knew the depths of the words they wrote, or if they knew how they might be interpreted in the future. I suspect they only partially understood.

Can non-Christians have intuitions when reading the Bible? Of course! But the difference is that Christians, who have been made alive in Christ (Ephesians 2) have intuitions that are drawn from a collection of all the insights and experiences we've had from God. We further build on these intuitions with surrounding biblical truths to protect any creative direction from becoming non-truth. Trusting your intuition or your 'gut feeling' becomes more reliable when you have layers of knowledge and revelation underneath the intuitions that God has previously established.

A non-Christian could read the Bible and explore any intuitions they have. But if they do this without inner intuitive guidance from the Holy Spirit and support from good Christian sources, and then decide to draw up conclusions from their own opinion, the result could be a bias-based intuition. This might not be a fair and trustworthy interpretation of scripture.

Storing your intuitions

What if you have some kind of intuition when reading the Bible, but you're not sure how to go about building it into something more fleshed out? You've prayed, read commentaries and studied the scripture in whatever way you can, but you're left feeling a little unsatisfied in a particular passage. Perhaps it will stay this way for now? Maybe those passages will become brighter on another day.

Or perhaps you give the scripture time to breathe into your life and ask the Spirit if He has anything to show you with those verses, taking the pressure off yourself.

While reading Psalm 141, I experienced this. Before reading, I decided to read with strong intentionality to hear from the Holy Spirit somehow. Being aware of Him, I went in with energy, actively listening and paying attention to Him. It can make all the difference having that spiritual run-up before you start. I read this Psalm of David:

"I call to you, Lord, come quickly to me; hear me when I call to you. May my prayer be set before you like incense; may the lifting up of my hands be like the evening sacrifice." Psalm 141:1-2 (NIV)

The first thing that stood out was the word *'incense'* so I stopped and contemplated what this meant. When we come to the word with a prepared heart, the intuition can come quickly. I read it again with the thought of incense in my mind.

"I call to you, Lord, come quickly to me; hear me when I call to you. May my prayer be set before you like incense; may the lifting up of my hands be like the evening sacrifice." Psalm 141:1-2 (NIV)

I was thinking that incense travels up to God like our prayers. The way incense is portrayed here is like an offering to God. So if I think of prayer as being like an offering to God, it makes me want to please God with my prayers, the same way that incense would have done by the priests in Old Testament times. It makes me want to present to Him a beautiful prayer that pleases Him and is according to His will. It shows me there is a relationship between prayer and incense.

I wanted to read it again because I felt there was more to take from it. You may know what it feels like to get a revelation, but also know what it feels like to give up in frustration knowing there was more. I read it a third time.

"I call to you, Lord, come quickly to me; hear me when I call to you. May my prayer be set before you like incense; may the lifting up of my hands be like the evening sacrifice." Psalm 141:1-2 (NIV)

It's like David is offering himself to God. After reading it this third time, the part that stood out was the word *'quickly'*. He needs God to come to him quickly, there's an urgency about this. David seems to acknowledge that he cannot do this on his own, so he raises his arms to God. It's like there are no materials or possessions in the world that can satisfy David here, he needs God alone, and quickly.

Then I considered that sometimes we may have an expectation of slowness in our prayers, as if it takes a while for God to hear or do anything. If you ever think God is slow to hear or slow to respond, that is not a Biblical idea. With this new thing to think about, I kept reading.

"I call to you, Lord, come quickly to me; hear me when I call to you. May my prayer be set before you like incense; may the lifting up of my hands be like the evening sacrifice." Psalm 141:1-2 (NIV)

So what was the Holy Spirit saying? The very faith-filled manner through which David is approaching God I think is pleasing to God. David knows he's only human, and he's weak without God. I'm thinking - what does this mean for us today?

But at this point when I was reading, I was getting tired of thinking. I was semi-satisfied by what I got from this verse, but not fully, I felt there was more. I felt that I needed to leave it there for that day because I was becoming lost in my thoughts almost. It's like I wasn't able to read it clearly anymore because I became too analytical in my head. At times, we can use our brain power too much when reading scripture. So what did I do? I was done for the day on these verses and closed the book – that was all I could do. Sometimes you need to give scripture room to breathe into your life, in the hope that something will be revealed someday.

What happened next?

A couple of days later, I was reading the book of Revelation and something caught my eye.

In Revelation 5 we have this scene where the apostle John is seeing a vision, and the scene is of God being on the throne in heaven. God is encircled by twenty-four elders and four living beings (don't worry if this doesn't mean anything to you). The scene progresses to a lamb (who represents Jesus) taking a scroll from God, and here, in this verse, John is describing what he sees:

"And when he took the scroll (Jesus as the Lamb)**, the four living beings and the twenty-four elders fell down before the Lamb. Each one had a harp, and they held gold bowls filled with incense,** (and here's the key) **which are the prayers of God's people"** Revelation 5:8 **(NLT)** (My notes added in brackets)

In this scene in heaven, God is surrounded by these twenty-four elders, and each one has a golden bowl filled with incense, produced by the prayers of God's people. And so of course I naturally thought back to Psalm 141- the verses I was reading a couple of days before, where it talked about incense, the first word that stood out when I read it.

Because I had read the two verses in Psalm 141 several times over and spent time considering them, they were held in my mind and close to my thoughts. And because I wasn't fully

Spiritual intuition

satisfied with my Psalm 141 reading, I felt that I had unfinished business with it. Therefore I started to see my life *through* the verses without even trying to remember them. Straight away I went back to Psalm 141 again with the fresh perspective I got from Revelation 5.

"I call to you, Lord, come quickly to me; hear me when I call to you. May my prayer be set before you like incense; may the lifting up of my hands be like the evening sacrifice." Psalm 141:1-2 (NIV)

Do you see it? Let me explain.

In this Psalm of David, he's talking about how his prayer is like incense, while he's on earth. Then in Revelation 5, John talks about how the prayers of God's people are bowls of incense before God, in heaven. That's amazing! It's like David's psalm is the earthly side of the prayer and in the book of Revelation, we see how the prayer has reached heaven in the form of incense, the very thing he was praying about! The prayer crosses from this dimension to another.

What does this mean for us today? It tells us that God hears our prayers, and He hears them quickly! To see this demonstrated in such a physical way adds a tangibility to our faith. What a comfort knowing this! When the Holy Spirit showed me this, I was so pleased! There's the life, there's the revelation, there's the kind of demonstration I hoped to show you. An intuition turned into a revelation.

Sometimes you might pray and feel like your words are just going into the air, that God *might* hear you and that He will get round to it at some point. No, He hears you the instant you pray, He hears before you even prayed in a sense. How would you feel if you gave up on praying at some stage in your life, to later find out that God was listening, that you have a bowl of incense in heaven, but it was only half-full? It's the fire in our hearts that ignites the prayers that God listens to, as the fire that burns the incense appearing in heaven.

Do you see how the Holy Spirit took me on this journey? I started with Psalm 141 - see how it developed! I had some kind of intuition that there was something in the words *prayer* and *incense*, but I couldn't quite bring it to a point where I felt satisfied. Like the young shepherd boy David, I was slinging stones with my head, using all my knowledge to hit the target, to force a revelation by my strength.

A couple of days later, the verse in Psalm 141 was called to my mind because of Revelation 5, which gave me a more dimensional understanding of Psalm 141. As David began slinging stones with his heart, it became effortless to hit the target, effortless for the revelation to come my way. I could never have planned for this to happen.

Having revelations about God is a collaboration with Him, we cannot do it on our own if we are to be deeply and spiritually satisfied. This is emphasised in the book of James where it says **"Draw near to God, and he will draw near to you" James 4:8 (ESV)**

Finding revelation

There are different things we can do with our intuitions and they can be followed in different ways. What happens when you come across scriptures that aren't moving you when you feel they could?

Well, we also read scripture to invest in future revelation as well as current. The same way you invest or save money for something important, even if you don't yet know what it's for. When we read scripture, sometimes we are investing in something that we might not understand yet - think of that glowing shepherd boy slinging stones to protect his sheep, unaware he is training to protect God's sheep.

The point here is that we take every intuition as far as we can, and do whatever we can to turn it into some kind of empowering revealing truth today. But if you cannot do it today, you've still moved it further along than it was before, so you can treat it as an investment for another day.

Picking up your Bible to start reading every day is the beginning, learning how to identify your intuitions and searching for the revelation they behold. A revelation from God when reading the Bible tends to be a certain spiritual distance away from us, a distance travelled by faith, not by sight (2 Corinthians 5:7).

Reading the Bible by following our intuitions can be a time where we are training on how to hear from God through His word, like a shepherd boy training to use his sling for something bigger than he currently understands. We learn head knowledge of various strategies, skills and methods to read the Bible, yes, as you will learn in this book. But they become more powerful when we let them go. They dissolve into our intuition and come back out emerging from us when we read the Bible with our hearts.

If you're like me, a person who used to read the Bible with such great frustration (I wanted to know everything, yet knew nothing and wasn't moved by anything), you may be close to experiencing a beautiful, liberating and creative freedom when reading the Bible, listening to the heart of God as if held in His arms. Let us walk further in...

Chapter Two
Revelation tactics

There is nothing more mind-blowing to experience in life than God's presence. It comes at different intensity's as the sun is hotter the closer you get to it. His word gives us an awareness of His presence and it's available on every page. Are you experiencing this with your Bible reading? Do you know how?

Getting revelations in your Bible reading is an important thing to have regularly as you walk with Jesus in your life. A revelation is an unveiling of truth that has a powerful resonance to you personally. They all seem to have commonalities in that they are exciting, empowering, emotional, educational and life-changing. But they all have their distinctiveness in their meanings and the level by which they impact you.

If you agree that all scripture is filled with revelation and that this can be mind-blowing, whether from experience or through your intuition, then how regularly are you experiencing it in your Bible reading?

Understanding scriptures and getting revelation from them are two different things. Knowledge on its own doesn't always have life functionality, whereas a revelation empowers and energises you to bear fruit. But a revelation is only a revelation when it becomes personal to you. I think that's why some people can talk about the Bible in an exciting passionate way while others cannot.

A revelation is not something you can necessarily choose to get in any given moment in your Bible reading. However it is something you can prepare for, something you can spend time working on by reading, re-reading, praying, researching, meditating and contemplating passages. These are things you can choose to do. But you cannot necessarily choose the moment that you get a revelation.

They say that *'luck is when preparation meets opportunity'*. I'll rephrase that and say *'revelation is when preparation meets the Holy Spirit'*. That means we prepare for revelation.

Over the centuries people seem to have found different ways to experience the eye-opening revelation that is available in scripture. They always seem to comprise the same kinds of things such as reading scripture, praying about the scripture, studying it, meditating on it and so on. People tend to mould these various ways of getting revelation into something that works for them. We see from all this, that there is a bridge to cross from the point at which you pick up the Bible, to the point at which you get revelation from it.

I want to help you put yourself in a stronger position so you can experience a broader range of eye-opening and life building moments when you read the Bible. So the idea is that we set our Bible reading up by preparing to receive lifelong revelation.

When people are serious about things in life, they tend to make plans to move quickly along their chosen path. I think that reading the Bible can and should be treated the same. If you agree that you will be reading the Bible for the rest of your life, then you would be smart to consider a strategy for how you are going to approach this journey.

I would like to present you with some general Bible reading tactics in this chapter. If some, or even none of these tactics resonate with you, then prayerfully consider that God can give you different strategies to get more out of the Bible. These, I hope, will put you in a stronger position to receive revelation in your Bible reading for the rest of your life.

Revelation tactic: Bible translations

Using different Bible translations is important. This can bring you to a place of satisfied understanding when reading and preparing for revelation. You can use these translations tactically. If you come across a passage that you intuitively feel you need to spend time on, aside from using Bible commentaries, exploring different translations can enable the flow of the Bible's life into yours.

There are two main kinds of Bible translations: *Word for word'* and *'meaning for meaning'*. *Paraphrases'*, not considered as translations, can be a very helpful aid when reading the Bible also.

'Word for word' is a literal translation: "This is what the original says, now how do we translate these words into English?". The intention is to stay as close to the meaning of the oldest and most original Greek and Hebrew manuscripts we have, translating each word into the closest English equivalent. They also keep the same sentence structure, although they might not always have the most smooth-flowing English that a *'meaning for meaning'* might have. The goal is to change as little as possible from the original. Examples include the *New American Standard Version* (NASB) and the *English Standard Version* (ESV).

'Thought for thought' or meaning for meaning: "This is what the Greek says, now how do we say that in English?". It attempts to identify the Greek meaning and find a similar English meaning. Thought for thought might use an English idiom not found in the literal Greek because that's the way you would express this idea in English. Examples include the *New International Version* (NIV) and the *New Living Translation* (NLT).

So *'Word for word'* translations focus on the vocabulary - Greek words into English words, while *'meaning-based'* translations take the Greek meaning into English using contemporary language.

'Paraphrases' are all about conveying the meaning of the original in a way that is easy to understand, and so an accurate translation is not important with these. Often they are written by one person (as opposed to translations, which is a careful team or group effort). Examples include *The Message* and *The Passion*.

My intention is not to exhaust the subject of translations, argue which is best or tell you to stay away from certain paraphrases, but to show or remind you that they are to be used as tools to help you. Different translations are like a set of tools that each do the same job, as ten different screwdrivers all do the same thing but each has its distinct feel. Perhaps get used to using one main translation, when you feel ready, try another. Use them to help you reel in a revelation.

Perhaps you could use a *pyramid method*, for any passages you find difficult to understand. This is where you first read it in a more literal *word for word* translation and consider what is being said. Go up the pyramid and read the same passage again in a *meaning for meaning* translation with more consideration. Then up to the top of the pyramid and read it in a *paraphrase* to help you see things in the passage you may have missed. You then go back down the pyramid reading the *meaning for meaning* and finishing back at the *word for word*. You could do the pyramid the other way round starting with a paraphrase or finding your own custom way of doing it. In and around this, try using Bible commentaries to expand your vision of what is being said. You're putting yourself in a stronger position to identify a revelation.

We use different translations to help us get more vibrancy out of the meaning. Sometimes you just run into a chapter that you know you need to spend time on, maybe a couple of days, and reading different translations often helps to unlock the things you might not be seeing. Sometimes our trust in God can hang on passages or verses we're struggling with, and so wise use of Bible translations can help to deal with our difficulties.

Revelation tactic: Investigate context

Any time you're starting a new book in the Bible it's a good idea to get in the right frame of mind for that particular book because this enables you to interpret what you're reading with more accuracy.

When you meet a new person, you learn about them from the outside and work your way in. You first see what they look like, you then get to know their name and eventually, after spending some time with them, you get to know their heart. When you deeply care about someone, you can begin to feel what they feel and understand why they do what they do.

This process is similar to getting to know God through the Bible. And so developing an understanding of context to access scripture happens in stages, from getting to know Him more and more through regular reading. To intimately understand God through scripture, get to know Him from the outside and then work your way in.

This means we start by learning the quick and easy, yet important information that helps us to frame the book we are about to read. The same as when you meet someone new, you first learn the quick and easy things, like their name, what they do, where they're from, to frame your thinking towards them.

In the Bible, this means learning things such as, who was the author of the book you're starting? Who was the audience they address? What was the purpose of the book? You need the date it was written, the genre and other important information to help you frame things and understand certain intricacies of the book. When you learn these introductory things, you then work your way into deeper levels of understanding after, such as character backgrounds, emotional dynamics and hidden meanings.

The people for whom the books of the Bible were first written, automatically had context because it was their history and their lives. So should we. As soon as you get this information, straight away you've parachuted yourself into a more appropriate frame of mind and set yourself up for more accurate insights. If you do it the other way round and try to understand highly emotional or intricate theological passages from books of which you have no contextual understanding, revelation is possible yes, but the subject matter and broadness of that revelation may be limited.

It is good, therefore, to find your favourite go-to resources to help you with the Bible. A Bible commentary is a person's thoughts and opinions on what the Bible is saying, verse for verse, written to help you understand it more. Some of which list the what, where, when and why type information that gives you the quick and easy context needed to know the background of a book. Many commentaries have been written over the centuries. Having a couple at hand for you to refer to is a fast track way to understand things that might otherwise take you hours.

Revelation tactic: Exploring your thoughts

Gaining revelation from scripture often comes through contemplation. When you have an intuition that there is some personal treasure in the scripture you're reading, though you're not clear on what it might be, then exploring this intuition may be the next step.

It's possible to learn so much from the Bible that you can forget what you know, so it's important to find practical ways to recall your knowledge. Through contemplation, the Holy Spirit can bring to remembrance what scripture says (John 14:26).

Sometimes when you contemplate a passage, you can get stuck in your thinking. You have a sense there is something powerful but your thoughts have kind of hit a dead end, and so therefore it is good to find ways of getting unstuck. I would always recommend a short prayer as the first thing you do here, but you still need to make an effort after the prayer has been made.

Conversations with people about the passage and their fresh perspective can open up your blind spots. Recording voice memos to get your thoughts down gives space for new thoughts. Closing your eyes to heighten your focus on a verse can give you the insight that you've intuitively become aware of. Taking advantage of all the amazing resources we have such as short videos or commentaries might be one of the quickest ways to uncover more of the goal of your intuition.

Creating an enabling environment for your reading is powerful and finding ways to keep things practical and efficient is also important. I think that if you have a strong desire to experience more power from the Bible, something as simple as organising practical things can move you closer to a revelation.

Revelation tactic: Linking scripture to your life

Jesus is always the conduit for scripture changing you and making you more holy, whether He is mentioned in the passages or not. If you're reading Old Testament scripture, aside from finding good moral lessons and teachings, how you bring it to relevance in your life today is by linking it to Jesus, and then the Holy Spirit can make it powerful and personal to you.

Why link it to Jesus? Because He is the very reason that we can have a personal relationship with God and therefore the power to apply scripture into our lives comes *through* Him, the living word.

But how does that work? Take the story of Noah's ark as an example. If you were trying to derive life lessons from it without considering Jesus, you might speak of how Noah was persevering and tenacious in building the ark in such difficult circumstances, and somehow *encourage yourself* to be like this too. But when you realise that Jesus is in the story as the ark itself, you see that Jesus was with Noah, He was the very source of his empowerment, perseverance and tenacity the whole time.

Think about the verses in the New Testament where Jesus talks about how our faith only needs to be the size of a mustard seed to move the mountains or difficulties in our lives (Matthew 17:20). He suggests we have the power to do things like this because the Holy Spirit is inside us and teaches us how to connect our circumstances to His promises. We link all scripture to Jesus for His endless and comprehensive empowerment to make it a reality. Without Him, any human empowerment is weak and unreliable.

Why do we need to link scriptures to ourselves? Because humans are driven partly by personal incentives. Underneath our desire to do the wrong things or act out of selfishness, we instinctively want restoration from such actions. If scripture does not become personal to us then it has no leverage to change us. People tend to enjoy hearing about the revelation that other people have received, but this is never as powerful as when you experience it for yourself.

So we link all scripture to Jesus so He can use it to restore us. The key to letting scripture change you is when the Holy Spirit makes it personal to you. So if you can come to a point where you acknowledge and believe that all scripture can be converted into relevance for us, through the power of Jesus and by the revelation of the Holy Spirit, then you will start to realise that all the pages in scripture can act as a personal mirror into your own life.

Revelation tactic: Read all the books in the Bible

The more scripture we have read overall, the Old as well as New Testaments, you start to see that deeper meaning from individual verses comes from knowing the Bible as a whole. It is a team effort of all the letters, the words, the verses, chapters and books that contribute to the experience of a revelation.

I am not suggesting that you have to read all the books in the Bible to get revelation, or that you have to do it to be on fire for God, not at all. But I'll ask you this, how much contextual information do you need to know to get a revelation?

Well, how much light do you need to light up a pitch-black room? A single lit match will reveal a lot about a dark room yes, but sixty-six lit matches (all the books of the Bible) will reveal more and more detail. Each book is like a lit match, each one reveals more about Jesus. So reading throughout the whole Bible is a smart tactic because of its interconnectedness and how all the books help to light each other up.

In my personal experience, some of the greatest revelations I have had from the Bible, have come from chapters that I thought were utterly irrelevant to my life, until I understood why they were important to me personally. No chapter in the Bible is for one specific time only, all chapters are for all eras and generations.

Above and beyond anything I say, let God lead you into the books you read. In time my friend, learn to read and love all scripture, even the parts you find boring. Over time, perhaps you could actively seek to understand and get revelation from the books in the Bible you don't like reading. This supplies more matches to light up areas of darkness in your life and the world around you. Through all this, we are helped to understand what things are like from His heart.

There is a culture among Christians of avoiding scriptures such as the book of Revelation, a mind-blowing book in the Bible that can breathe life in you today. It's not just about interesting things that may or may not occur in the future and have no use for you today.

How different do you feel today because of the ideas and plans you have for the future? Your ideas and plans affect the decisions you make today. The book of Revelation has a similar effect in that it has the power to change the way you live today because it teaches you about what is to come in the future.

It is therefore exceptionally relevant if you learn how to navigate or link the truth into your life. By faith, we can learn about what happens in the future, giving us Gods miraculous perspective now.

The book of Revelation is just an example similar to other commonly avoided books. I think God planned that the Bible as a whole should give us a variety of books that give us balance in our beliefs, with great access and potential to develop Jesus' character in us.

To summarise

When you get to know someone and develop a love for them, you begin to feel what they feel. When they find things funny, you find those same things funny, because you want to share their heart, and you want to feel what they feel. This happens over time because you've gotten to know them, learned about their life, their background, their passions, their pains, their desires. You've learned their context.

We approach our Bible reading as if it's a person we are getting to know and a person we could eventually love, that person being God. To learn the beauty of God, to see things from His perspective, to feel what He feels, to feel joy when He does and to feel His anger. You get to know Him in part, by understanding the scripture you're reading and reading every part of it, even the parts you're not so keen on. In time, you will see that revelation is available in every part of scripture. We just need to prepare for it.

These are general tactics to set the right temperature to receive more of Him. In the rest of the chapters, I will show you more specific ways to move closer to the heart of God.

Chapter Three

Inner biblical interpretation & handling your doubts about God

The way you interpret scripture directly affects the way you understand God, which directly affects the understanding of your life purpose. So we want to, as best as we can, interpret scriptures, to release the life they hold into our life. If you have difficulties with many scriptures and persevere to overcome these, you will be released to grow exponentially.

The greatest source by which we can interpret scripture is scripture itself. We call this *'inner-biblical interpretation'*. Each book understood on its own with no other understanding of other books in the Bible, is of great value. But each book understood with reference to the other books in the Bible, then becomes more clear, relevant and more profoundly life-giving.

The books work together

We would be left with too many questions if you were reading the book of Job and that was all we had. But because we've got an entire body of scripture that gives us more of a view into the spiritual realm, more of a view into suffering and more of a view into miracles, then all of sudden, we can navigate Job within the context of the whole Bible.

Take the book of Leviticus for example - we can navigate that book and it becomes life-giving because we see it in the context of the whole Bible. And then we appreciate all the more the sacrifice of Christ and the forgiveness of sins because we see the back end mechanics of it through the Levitical priesthood, how they dealt with sin, impurities and uncleanliness.

So an individual Bible book cannot be seen in isolation if we are to gain a better understanding of it. All the individual words in the Bible have life in them. But that life comes only from understanding the sentence in which they are contained. The same also with the sentence, life in the sentence is added from understanding it in relation to its paragraph and chapter. It's the same with the chapter. Life in the chapter is added from understanding it in the context of the book. And the significance of the book comes from understanding it in the context of the whole sixty-six books.

God has interconnectedness built within all His creation. At the physical level, our muscles do not work in isolation, they work together as a team. At the level of society, people thrive better together, as a team. The Bible is woven cohesively, in that all the books work together so that they give you a deeper understanding of each other. So the greatest commentary on the Bible is the Bible itself.

The New Testament has over a thousand references from the Old Testament, and it sheds more light on those verses when you go back to them in the Old Testament. And so much of the Old Testament will seem irrelevant to you unless you read it within the bigger picture of the New.

The book of Leviticus read on its own, with no understanding of the other books, will seem utterly irrelevant for you today. It's a book about God's holiness and the conditions required for His people to approach Him – before the birth of Jesus. If you have an understanding of some New Testament scripture, such as Hebrews, Romans or the Gospels, this, along with guidance from the Holy Spirit, can unlock your ability to navigate Leviticus so that it becomes utterly life-giving for you today.

In the New Testament, if you read the book of Revelation with no understanding of any other Bible books, you will probably find it hopeless to understand what's going on. It's a book about Christ being unveiled to His people and the events building up to His second coming. Reading Old Testament books like Daniel, Isaiah and the Gospels along with guidance from the Holy Spirit and help from Bible resources such as commentaries or videos, will help you to better interpret more of what Revelation has to say.

The books I have mentioned so far are just a couple of examples that may or may not mean anything to you right now. But with *'inner-biblical interpretation'* we can let the Bible interpret itself to us. Any good Bible resources you use to help you, whether videos or books, will always go by this principle.

Is God of the Old Testament evil?

What if you run into great difficulty? Maybe a moral difficulty you have or some doubt about God. I've got one for you as an example, many people have difficulties with this. In 1 Samuel 15:2-3, the prophet Samuel, the advisor to King Saul of Israel, said the following to the King:

"This is what the LORD Almighty says: 'I will punish the Amalekites for what they did to Israel when they waylaid them as they came up from Egypt. Now go, attack the Amalekites and totally destroy all that belongs to them. Do not spare them; put to death men and women, children and infants, cattle and sheep, camels and donkeys.'" 1 Samuel 15:2-3 (NIV)

This scripture (among other similar stories) has caused difficulties for people with the Bible. It's scriptures like this that make people think the God of the Old Testament is evil and the God of the New Testament is loving. But when you navigate your way to other parts of scripture, you start to understand why God would command such a thing. And as crazy as it might seem, you can see that this command was just and totally loving.

Maybe you have a mistrust of God because of your interpretation of a woman's place in the church based on Paul's writings. Maybe you mistrust God because of your interpretation of homosexuality in the Bible.

If you had a suspicion about the integrity of a friend or partner, would you not want to ask them about it, to give a better chance of trusting them? Then how much more important is your relationship with God? You could fold your arms and decide to never deal with any mistrust you have for God or the Bible, or you could take time to handle your difficulty with care.

Let me attempt to explain the difficulty of these verses from 1 Samuel 15. Why did God command the genocide of the Amalekite people? I will explain this by using inner-biblical interpretation.

Here we go

God's thoughts are bigger than our thoughts, His ways are bigger than our ways (Isaiah 55:9). He is all-knowing, not only does He see all things that happen today, He sees all things that happen in the future.

And in this situation, God knew what would happen if the Amalekites were not completely wiped out. He knew what would happen in the future. If the Israelite army did not carry out God's orders, the Amalekites would come back in the future to cause Israel serious issues that would not only affect them but also you and me today.

After Samuel the prophet gave this command, later on in 1 Samuel 15:20, King Saul claimed that he had completely destroyed the Amalekites, except for their king, Agag. But still, further down the story, we see that Saul was either lying or deluded when he said this. A couple of decades later we see that in 1 Samuel 30:1-2, there were enough Amalekites to take David, the future king of Israel, and all his men's families captive. When David and his men escaped and rescued their families, David fought the Amalekites and four hundred of their young men escaped (1 Samuel 30:17). So if Saul had done what God originally commanded, this would never have happened.

So far we've stayed within 1 Samuel and Isaiah 55:9 to gain some context. Now I'll take you to another book to get even more understanding.

Several hundred years after the events in 1 Samuel, we see in the book of Esther that there is a man called Haman, who was a descendant of Agag king of the Amalekites. This Haman attempted the genocide of the Jews, a full extermination (ever noticed how often the devil tries to copy God's moves after Him?).

Saul's disobedience to God's command could have resulted in the destruction of Israel several hundred years later, because the life of Haman shows that Amalekites had not been totally destroyed. God then worked through an incredible woman named Esther to stop the genocide of the Jews through this wicked man.

God being God, all-knowing, knew that this would happen when He originally commanded Saul to take out the Amalekites, which seems to be why He commanded them to be wiped out.

More importantly than all this, even later down the line in history, as we see in the Gospels, Jesus the Messiah was born (Matthew 2:1), through David's family line as a direct descendant of the nation of Israel. Saul failing to fulfil God's command might seem to be an indirect attack from the devil to kill Jesus' ancestors so that Jesus would never be born. Throughout the Bible there are many times that the devil tried to kill off Jesus' ancestors, if he had succeeded, we would have no means of salvation today.

On top of this, the Amalekites were a horrific nation. Now we know that horrific people can turn to God and they can be saved through Christ. So couldn't some of the Amalekites have turned to God before He commanded their death?

We see throughout other parts of scripture the lengths God will go to for the sake of one righteous person let alone a nation. For the sake of anyone who would turn to Him, such as Noah and his family (Genesis 6), Lot and his family in Sodom and Gomorrah (Genesis 18 & 19), Rahab and her family (Joshua 6). As far as we know, there were none among the Amalekites. But what about the women, children and infants it mentions in 1 Samuel 15:2-3?

They may seem innocent to us but it doesn't mean they *are* innocent. God sees the bird's eye view. If these Amalekite children had grown up to learn what Israel had done to their families, they may have sought revenge and continued to war against them, permitting the devil to kill the seed of Jesus.

However I acknowledge it's not entirely fair to assume they would do this, but God knows, and He saw it as just to remove them. You might argue that if Israel didn't attack them, there may have been peace. But we see throughout scripture that the Amalekites intention was always to destroy and they were governed by sinister practices, God knew what He was doing. If God gives life, we cannot question Him if He decides to take it. By His just and loving nature, this will always be the right decision.

To add to this, in other scripture such as 2 Samuel 12:23, David seems to indicate that when children or infants die before the age of being accountable before God, they go to the Lord, meaning that it is likely there are Amalekites in heaven. And in light of the inconceivable awesomeness of heaven, isn't it possible that they go there early?

And what about the *"cattle and sheep, camels and donkeys"* mentioned in 1 Samuel 15:2-3 which God asks Saul to wipe out? How on earth can you justify this?

There are not enough reasons to believe that God would command such things unless they were justifiable, it's not congruent with what scripture says as a whole. It seems that there was a specific and irreversible reason that these animals needed to be wiped out. Information on this is sparse. But it has been said that the Amalekites had vampire-like practices with drinking blood. Perhaps this is why God felt the need to forbid this to Israel in the law (Leviticus 17:14) and to not be influenced by other nations during difficult times wandering in the desert. So it is possible the Amalekites had certain unclean practices with animals (Leviticus 20:15) that corrupted them on a genetic or spiritual level (Mark 5:13) to the point of no return, as opposed to being the happy farm animals we might imagine. God commanding this suggests something went wrong with them. I think as Christians who trust God, this does not tend to be a problem because of the broader trust we have in Him, but, it can be a difficulty for seekers or non-believers.

We do see all over scripture how God is just. So if you see Him doing something that appears to be unjust, of course, you could just say He is a horrible God and leave it at that, as often many people do. Or you could investigate another reason and handle an important issue that could be holding back your love for Him.

With that consistent theme of God being just, killing

people off might (as we have seen) actually be just also, if you see the bigger picture. And in light of all this, the command to take out the Amalekites might have been, the most loving act, in disguise. I think if there were anyone who would be truly heartbroken that this was the best way, then it would be God.

Often, as with this example, you will need to reference other parts of the Bible to bring satisfaction to the part you're on. You use the clear parts of scripture to help you understand the unclear parts. 1 Samuel 15:2-3 on its own, leaves us with too many questions. But when you read further on in Samuel, read the book of Esther, read parts of the Gospels, read some of Genesis or Joshua as explained, then you will be able to navigate a potential misunderstanding and mistrust of God, to get to a place where you trust Him more than ever.

And I find that when you look at all your difficulties on a case by case basis, there is always a just and fair answer to show that God was right. When you do this enough it helps you to see that He can be fully trusted. Inner biblical interpretation releases us into a more trusting and loving relationship with God.

If you go to see a life coach, one of the things they will do is help you to see things in a positive light, so you leave the session feeling full of life. They dispel the lies you've told yourself that bring you down and cause you to feel worthless. How much more is your own identity in God strengthened when you carefully work through and handle your difficulties in the Bible? Use the Bible, to interpret the Bible, to trust God more and find a greater sense of identity in Him.

The way I look at it, the quicker you can get a good level of biblical understanding and trust in God the better, because you have more of your life to enjoy this trust. Rather than waiting till years later, saving it for your time off work, or for your retirement, for whatever reason, the longer you leave it, the less time you'll have to enjoy it. You get one life, if you want to live it to the full, you find a way to trust God and what He has said.

How do we go about using this inner biblical interpretation strategy?

Aside from using Bible resources to help you, using mega themes to help with inner-biblical interpretation is one of the ways we can do this. So we interpret the unclear parts of scripture, by using the clear parts, to help us gain the clarity we need. Mega themes in the Bible are a handy way to do this. A mega theme is a theme or truth of some sort that is consistent throughout the whole Bible.

One of the mega themes in the Bible that comes across through all the books is that God is just, He's absolutely just. It's a thing that appears in so many places that many believers don't tend to even need to look for a verse to tell them because it's a general theme, a mega theme that is throughout the Bible. There are many verses and stories that demonstrate this.

One of my favourite examples demonstrating the theme of God's justness is to read the law, which is spread through the books of Exodus, Leviticus, Numbers and Deuteronomy. Reading them has the powerful effect of reminding you of the perfection of God's standard, how fair and how loving He is.

This means then that if you find anything in the Bible that might appear as an injustice from God, you then have to compare this apparent injustice with the fact that the Bible consistently demonstrates that God is just. You could argue that there's the odd exception and that sometimes God gets it wrong, and then move on from that part as if you've made up your mind. But in light of what scripture says as a whole, that's not a fair assessment. Things like this can hold back your love for God, which will always reflect on your own life.

Take the apparent injustice that God seems to have committed, and in light of the mega theme of God's justness, then consider that He might have actually been just in this situation, and there has to be another way to explain what happened. At least this is a way you can start the process of understanding it.

Now over time from reading scripture, and working your way through difficulties such as 1 Samuel 15:2-3, you start to notice the pattern that God is totally just. You start to realise that God being perfectly just is a very important mega theme in scripture that helps you to navigate your way through other unclear scriptures you come across later on.

Using mega themes as the starting point to explore our difficulties

In the instance of 1 Samuel 15:2-3, where we found this difficult scripture, the formula that we follow is to take the truth that is clear from all through the rest of scripture, that God is just. Then we use this solid and consistent truth (or mega theme) as a gateway to navigate through those particular difficult verses in 1 Samuel 15, to a satisfactory understanding.

It appeared that God wanting to exterminate a tribe of people was wrong, that's how it looks in our humanness. Because we apply our human thinking and logic to the situation, we conclude that God was wrong here and sometimes forget that God's ways are higher than ours.

But when you use the fact that God is so just in so many places in the Bible, you then use this to filter out the possibility that He was wrong. This then forces us to look at the difficult verses differently and search for the possibility that He may have been right. We can't just look at the verses anymore and say that God was wrong or unjust. It's simply not fair to say that, especially when you look at His character all over the Bible (such as my example from reading the law).

If you know a person well and know them to be a person of high integrity (because they've demonstrated this consistently for years), but then one day see them extremely angry about something, you will more than likely assume that their anger is justifiable and that they are angry for the right reasons. You base this assumption on the fact that you know them to be of great character, as opposed to assuming they are angry due to any immoral or indefensible reason. And when you get to see God's character throughout scripture, it gives you the heart and confidence to approach the difficulties with more reason.

To take this further still, we use a second mega theme in the Bible to help us more, to help us get perspective. This time, that God is *all-knowing*. In Luke 12:7 Jesus tells us how God knows the number of hairs on your head, which is a truth in itself but more importantly, it illustrates that God knows everything. So in the instance of 1 Samuel 15, we have to then consider that God knows more than we do, including everything that will happen in the future. This then, looking at our previous example, points to everything we see in the book of Esther when Haman tries to kill the Jews. God knew this would happen back in 1 Samuel 15.

We then take yet another mega theme in the Bible to help us with 1 Samuel 15, a third mega theme, and this is important. God is all-loving. The most loving act that has ever happened in history is when He sent Jesus, His own innocent and Holy son to take the punishment so that we don't have to. Christians call this the *'good news'*. And in light of this, we are then forced to consider that God giving this command to Saul, to kill off a nation, is somehow actually a loving thing. Again, to say God was evil here, in light of what we know about Him elsewhere throughout scripture, is unreliable and unfair.

So we use these three particular mega themes or mega truths about God, truths that are consistent and clear throughout all scripture. His justness, His all-knowingness, and His all-lovingness, as ways to filter out any possible option that God was wrong or immoral. This then forces us to consider that God commanding the Amalekite destruction was actually the right thing to do at that time and in that place, because He is just, all-knowing and all-loving. Using this strategy of mega themes may not give us detailed answers right away, but it starts the process.

In this particular instance, the rest of the Bible shows us why God was right to have made this command to kill off the Amalekites. We see from other scriptures such as the book of Esther, that Haman, who came from the escaped Amalekites, tried to kill all the Jews. Then, when Jesus (who was a Jew) was born, everyone was enabled to come to God through Him, and He now inhabits spiritually in the lives of Christians today.

So we use the characteristics or attributes that God demonstrates throughout the Bible, these mega themes, to help us deal with apparent contradictions or difficulties. That's one formula you can use.

Any time you see God doing something that surprises you in the Bible, you've got to hold it in your mind with His established characteristics as the starting point, to help you navigate to a place of truth. This will show you and even force you to look at it differently. I would advise you do this in tandem with commentary references to make life easier.

Using Jesus to help with inner biblical interpretation

Every single book and chapter in the Bible points to Jesus in the sense that they all teach you things about Him, either in an indirect way where He is in the story or a direct way where it is plainly speaking about Him.

In the New Testament, it's obvious that all the books talk about Jesus because they are always saying His name or referring to Him directly. In the Old Testament, while the stories were historical events, God in His power demonstrated Jesus in them, in that they act as spiritual demonstrations to show what Jesus would do when He came, and sometimes show Jesus present even before His birth.

So each book whether it is from the Old or New Testament, is like a lit match that illumines a different aspect of Jesus. And when all these books are understood through Him, your understanding of Him is illuminated, it shows you the depth of what He did for us on the cross.

However, I get that if you read an Old Testament book, it might not be the easiest thing to spot Jesus in all the stories when you haven't first learned about Him more directly in the New Testament.

Jesus is always the stepping stone between the Old Testament stories and your life today. Each Old Testament book in the Bible *without* Jesus might not mean much to you and me today, they're hidden, kind of irrelevant. They may just come across as interesting wise stories similar to other literature, as many non-Christians would think. Jesus is needed to illuminate these books and show you the real power behind them. Jesus is one of the best tools to help you with inner-biblical interpretation.

Try it yourself

How do you know when is the right time to use inner-biblical interpretation? Well with most of the chapters in this book it's fairly clear when to apply the strategies. You may want to use this one whenever you come across a personal difficulty in scripture, or if you want to gain a broader understanding of certain passages.

Use your tools to do this. Bible commentaries will often have a referencing system, listing other verses and stories in the Bible that relate and dig further into the passage you are reading. But to just get this principle into your Bible reading, to get it in your thinking, may well be enough for now. And then, reading and grasping more of scripture, interpreting the Bible from inside the Bible, will just start to come as a natural thing.

In the introduction of this book, I mentioned that God took the kingdom from Saul because of his disobedience. In light of what I have just talked about from 1 Samuel 15, we can see why, and why God sought out someone after His own heart to replace Saul. We move closer into God's heart when we learn to trust Him more and more. When you see how beautifully woven His word is, you begin to see that it is all you need to learn about Him, it's all in one place.

Your love for God flows easier when trust is there, so I strongly encourage you to handle any doubts you have about God and His word. Every book in the Bible complements every book in the Bible. Over time from doing this, you start to see that the best commentary on the Bible, is the Bible itself.

Chapter Four
Becoming the book author/ original readers

In many TV dramas, you have a particular main story going on that is often involving many characters and produces a certain feel and a certain emotional dynamic. Often, these dramas give you backstories of the lives of the individual characters, so that when it comes back to the main story, you then have a much deeper connection to them all, to the point where you begin to care about them. Because you have this background information from their individual stories, it means you start to see certain details in their actions. You begin to realise why these characters behave the way they do.

You can do a similar thing when reading the Bible, which is full of some of the most interesting and famous people in history. I want to show you the effectiveness of seeing things from the perspectives of the original authors and the original readers of the books of the Bible (when I say original readers or receivers, I mean the people whom the individual Bible books were first originally intended for). Reading from either of these perspectives puts you in the frame of mind to see layers of detail that can easily be missed. When you begin to understand the author's heart and the perspective of the original readers, you delve into a deeper understanding of God's heart.

Here is an example from 2 Timothy

I want to do something with you here. I want us to read a passage from the book of 2 Timothy. I'm going to give you very little context for the passage for this first reading. Then after we've read it, I'm going to give you some detailed context about the book's author Paul, and the book's intended reader Timothy.

After this, we will read it a second time. I want to see if you notice a difference in the way you feel about the book in light of the contextual information I'm going to give you.

Now can I ask that when you read the following passage in your head, or out loud, that you 'hear' it in a fairly flat tone? A tone that suggests you don't have a great deal of context and therefore you cannot put any particular emphasis on the way it is written and what you are hearing. (If you already know the immediate context of this passage, then this particular exercise might not be so powerful for you, however, you can use it as an example elsewhere in the Bible).

Before reading it this first time, here's a very small amount of context: Paul was writing this letter to a younger church leader named Timothy, and in this letter, Paul is giving him advice. That's all the context I'm going to give you for this first reading.

"But you must remain faithful to the things you have been taught. You know they are true, for you know you can trust those who taught you. You have been taught the holy Scriptures from childhood, and they have given you the wisdom to receive the salvation that comes by trusting in Christ Jesus. All Scripture is inspired by God and is useful to teach us what is true and to make us realize what is wrong in our lives. It corrects us when we are wrong and teaches us to do what is right. God uses it to prepare and equip his people to do every good work.

I solemnly urge you in the presence of God and Christ Jesus, who will someday judge the living and the dead when he comes to set up his Kingdom: Preach the word of God. Be prepared, whether the time is favourable or not. Patiently correct, rebuke, and encourage your people with good teaching.

For a time is coming when people will no longer listen to sound and wholesome teaching. They will follow their own desires and will look for teachers who will tell them whatever their itching ears want to hear. They will reject the truth and chase after myths.

But you should keep a clear mind in every situation. Don't be afraid of suffering for the Lord. Work at telling others the Good News, and fully carry out

the ministry God has given you." 2 Timothy 3:14 to 4:5 (NLT)

Consider how you felt when reading this. Maybe you didn't feel much? Maybe you did. I know when I read something with no context, it's not the most colourful of reads. When I read this with no context I enjoy it, it's good advice, but perhaps void of any strong and provocative emotion. Now, before we read it again, I'm going to give you more context on this passage.

Author of 2 Timothy: Paul wrote this letter near the end of his life while in his 60s. At this point he had been in Christian ministry for around 25-30 years, experiencing all kinds of things, including many near-death and violent experiences, to the point that his physical body would have been covered in all sorts of scars. And this is a letter that Paul wrote to his young protégé Timothy, who was like a spiritual son to him. 2 Timothy is one of the last letters Paul wrote. And here's one of the key points to put you in his shoes: he knew while writing this alone from prison in Rome, that he was going to be martyred soon. He was going to be killed because of his faith in Jesus. Knowing that gives you important foreknowledge which then illuminates many things in this letter and indeed these verses. This letter contains Paul's final instructions to this young church leader.

Original reader of 2 Timothy: Timothy was an overseer of the church in Ephesus and likely came to faith after Paul's first missionary tour. They were very close - it's possible that Timothy was led to Jesus by Paul. If you have ever led someone to God or were led to God by a particular person, you will know how special that relationship will always be. Timothy was a young church leader with a lot of responsibility and may have been looked down upon because of his age. He may not have had many people to encourage him.

Paul is giving so much advice and wisdom to Timothy that there's a sense of urgency in this letter. He wants to make sure he leaves something behind before he is martyred. It would be hard to see these things unless you understood this context beforehand.

Maybe you've loved someone who's shown similar behaviour like Paul towards the end of their life, and they wanted to make sure you were going to be okay before they passed. Maybe you are that older person now, you know what it feels like to be near the end of your life and you want to leave something behind.

I once watched a TV drama about a man who had recently lost his wife to cancer. In the show, you see that before the woman died, she filmed lots of little videos to instruct her husband on how to live his life. How to take care of himself, when to take the bins out and when to feed the dog. He watched these videos after she died, doing all the things she had said. It was very moving to watch. I think this letter to Timothy has a similar vibe: Paul giving final instructions to his son before he was killed. I wouldn't have been prompted to think of this TV drama had I not known the context of 2 Timothy. Thinking of your own way to relate to the passage works powerfully.

Become the author or reader

So here's what I suggest, read this as if you were Timothy, or write this as if you were Paul. I don't mean literally write out these verses (although you could try this) but think about writing it and how you might feel in Paul's circumstances. Try not to read it with both perspectives at the same time, choose either the author's or reader's perspective.

Unlike last time, where I suggested you read it in an emotionally flat way, this time I suggest you read with the emotion you would be feeling in light of the context you now have. Emphasise the intonation and read it at an appropriate speed. When you read messages from people, do you hear that person's voice in your mind? Well, if you're reading as Timothy, perhaps put on Paul's voice in your mind. What's Paul's voice like? We don't know, but you could read it with the voice of your own father or a father-like figure in your life.

Paul is a man who will soon be executed, writing his final instructions to his spiritual son whilst in prison. Paul at times may have been the only person Timothy had to support and guide him, so receiving a letter from him would be exciting and encouraging. How would you feel if you were Paul or Timothy?

Take a moment to get into the right character, put yourself in that context, and read to feel every ounce of emotion you can. Imagine writing these words as Paul, or reading these words as Timothy.

"But you must remain faithful to the things you have been taught. You know they are true, for you know you can trust those who taught you. You have been taught the holy Scriptures from childhood, and they have given you the wisdom to receive the salvation that comes by trusting in Christ Jesus. All Scripture

is inspired by God and is useful to teach us what is true and to make us realize what is wrong in our lives. It corrects us when we are wrong and teaches us to do what is right. God uses it to prepare and equip his people to do every good work.

I solemnly urge you in the presence of God and Christ Jesus, who will someday judge the living and the dead when he comes to set up his Kingdom: Preach the word of God. Be prepared, whether the time is favourable or not. Patiently correct, rebuke, and encourage your people with good teaching.

For a time is coming when people will no longer listen to sound and wholesome teaching. They will follow their own desires and will look for teachers who will tell them whatever their itching ears want to hear. They will reject the truth and chase after myths.

But you should keep a clear mind in every situation. Don't be afraid of suffering for the Lord. Work at telling others the Good News, and fully carry out the ministry God has given you." 2 Timothy 3:14 to 4:5 (NLT)

Can you see the difference between our first and second readings of these verses? It's powerful when you do it the second way. And it's even more powerful if you've been reading Paul's letters for months on end just before reading this letter. Over that time you have probably built up care for him, as with the characters in a TV drama. Have you ever cried because someone died in a TV show? We have great richness in the Bible to move us emotionally. In this example, it's like the end of an adventure for Paul, but the start of a new one for Timothy.

Dual emotionality

When you do this, you see that there is a dual emotionality to the Bible books. Throwing a ball is totally different from catching it, as is the emotion in the intention of the author and the emotion in the response of the reader. Two very different perspectives give two very different experiences.

I understand that people will have different experiences from my example. The context I gave about Paul and Timothy, may or may not be enough for you. But over time, when you get to know people more in the Bible, if you use this strategy, this type of emotional engagement will happen more often and at a deeper level, rather than me giving you a forced example. My intention is more to teach you a strategy for your Bible reading - should you ever feel the need to use it.

When you read or write through the perspective of the reader or author, it gives you two totally different experiences of the book, to the extent that you may see things that would otherwise be invisible. And that's the keyword here, invisible. There are many things in the Bible you're just not going to see unless you have background information. I think you can only go so far without knowing these details.

Where do you get information about the authors/readers?

Finding an overview video of your current Bible book online, or using a study Bible to look at character profiles may be the easiest way to start. Look at the specific historical circumstances surrounding the period of writing. I also find that over the years, as you read the Bible, you start to fill in more and more blanks about the authors and original readers as you go, giving you more vibrancy in the books you're reading. It's good to have your favourite sources to use as tools to get this kind of information quickly and easily.

Some principles to go by

So now that I have given you an example, let me explain this a little further. If you ever want to use this strategy to reveal layers of detail, you don't strictly have to read from both perspectives (author and intended reader), potentially exhausting yourself along the way. You could choose just one perspective. Do whatever you feel compelled to.

As another example, it is generally agreed upon that Moses wrote the first five books of the Bible, with the nation of Israel intended as the original readers/receivers for each one. But the fifth of these books, Deuteronomy, while still being addressed to Israel, was intended for the new generation that grew up in the desert, as opposed to the generation that grew up in Egypt, and died in the desert.

So, when reading from the perspective of this new generation, as opposed to the old (the ones who experienced the

Exodus, the giving of the law and so on), straight away your experiential surroundings change. Why? Because you're now reading from the perspective of the new generation raised under the disgruntled and pessimistic culture of the old generation. A generation who had only heard of, not experienced the Exodus or giving of the law, a generation who mostly experienced God-given food. How much does that change the way you feel when reading Deuteronomy? It changes everything.

But there are some things you should know first

There are some things to consider if you want to stay as theologically accurate as possible using this strategy, to understand the lives of the book authors and original readers.

Authors: Some of the books in the Bible have a definite and accepted author (because the book begins with the author's name in the introduction). With other books, there is some debate on authorship and in some cases, new theories of authorship emerge. To add to this, some books have more than one author.

Original readers/receivers: It may be a little easier to figure out the identities of the original readers of the books, if so, we may have fewer problems here. The readers or receivers tend to either be a specific group of people, such as the nation of Israel or specific, geographically located churches. Alternatively, the intended reader might be an individual, as in the case of Paul's co-workers Timothy and Titus.

If you prefer to stick with the books that have a clear author and specific reader for this strategy, then go with that.

There are more than enough of them to justify this as a strategy you can use in your reading.

How far you want to take this is up to you. You can study as much information as you can get your hands on to develop an understanding of both author and reader perspectives. Or you could spend a short time reading for context about the book's author and readers, using commentaries or videos online. Many of you may already know of some Bible book authors and readers, and therefore you might prefer to just read the books holding this awareness in your mind rather than doing any extra work.

We all have our limits as to what a life-giving study or a life-draining study might be, you will know how much is enough for you. Life-draining studies are no fun, so you could quite easily spend just a few minutes getting some information from Bible commentaries to put you in the right frame of mind for approaching the author and reader for that particular book and time period.

It is good to gain a general understanding of the author and original readers of the book you are about to read. For example, the Apostle Paul, you can find an overview of his life which will help you when reading any of the letters he wrote. You can also get a general overview of the original readers for whom he wrote.

But, to make our reading more relevant and specific for each and every book, we can learn about the circumstances of the author and their intended readership during the time and place of that particular book as best as we can.

Why is this a powerful way for us to read today?

Because it puts you in a refreshed, updated and relevant position, better allowing you to experience the emotional timeline that God sees, and edging us closer to understanding His heart more.

Moses's birth did not come until the book of Exodus, so he saw and experienced most of what happened in the books of Exodus, Leviticus, Numbers and Deuteronomy. He didn't live through what he wrote about in the book of Genesis. Reading from his perspective, you know that there will be a change in the feel of Genesis in comparison to the four books that come after. Also, because of the chronological progression from Exodus to Deuteronomy, you will become aware of Moses's personal experience and growth as he collects new memories during the progression of the books and the development of the story.

I don't necessarily expect you to go back and read the five books from these different perspectives, the idea is to show you that you can, I want to show you that advanced strategies are not only for scholars.

I'll point out that some Bible books will not be as straightforward as others with this particular strategy, due to a lack of available information about the authors and readers. But more importantly, I think there is significance in merely being aware that you can indeed try this approach with many of the books.

Books written to individuals or groups

Some books are written to individuals, while others are written to groups of people. 2 Timothy was written to one person while the first 5 books of Moses were written to a nation.

Have you ever written a message to one person, and in so doing conveyed your personal relationship with them through writing in a certain way? Adding certain specifics to what you say, speaking of a memory you both share, perhaps using certain personal language?

Have you written a message to a larger group of people? Writing in a more general yet inspiring way, covering topics that need to be explained in a way that many people can understand.

Why is this important? Because every book in the Bible has a distinct feel. Sometimes that is based largely on whether the author was writing to one person or a group. Just being aware of this with the book we are reading puts us in a more open frame of mind.

Reading from the perspective of different classes & cultures

If a letter was written to a nation or class of people, rather than an individual whose personal details we have, then how can we read from their perspective? Well, we can make an educated guess based on our understanding of an average person within that class and the kinds of things that define that class.

What do you know about Gentiles back then? (Gentiles are non-Jewish people) Or what do you know about Jewish people back then? Reading scripture over the years teaches you more about both and indeed others. This helps you to step into their shoes when reading a book that has their culture in mind, and thus enables you to understand the language of a particular book better.

If reading from the perspective of converted Gentiles in church groups, the main original readers for most of Paul's letters, you will have grown up without knowing the true God and without knowing your identity in Him. Celibacy, for example, might never have entered your mind until recently. You grew up without having the same level of peace that you've recently been experiencing. You grew up without knowing where you came from, not understanding forgiveness, or knowing much about where you go after you die. Paul skilfully helps Gentile believers catch up on these topics in his letters so they can understand the meaning of the cross in depth.

Jews on the other hand grew up with more clarity on these things. If reading from the perspective of a Jewish convert, books such as Matthew, James, Hebrews and most of the Old Testament (written predominantly with Jews in mind) will make more sense because of your foundations. So a Jewish person reading Matthew for the first time (which starts with a family tree of famous Jewish people) will find it easier to understand than a Gentile, who knows nothing of these people.

We get a better handle on living from the heart of God when we see scripture from the perspective of Jews, Gentiles, Samaritans, Pharisees curious about Jesus, idol worshippers and so on. This can show us the broad power and universality of the cross. As well as redeeming us before God, the cross empowers us, remember that.

To summarise

How far you use a technique like this is up to you. You can do a deep contextual study, a quick one that takes a couple of minutes, or start with what you already know and have an awareness of the author and reader's perspectives. My intention is not to exhaust this subject, but rather to show you that this is something you can do.

If you are Timothy reading Paul's letter for the first time, you will be excited to hear from your spiritual father. Texts, emails and phone calls were not around back then, a letter was a rare thing. But when you (from Timothy's perspective) get to 2 Timothy 4:6, you will be deeply shaken and moved when you find out what it says about Paul's impending death. When you regroup and re-read the letter again (still as Timothy) the second reading will be very different and you will understand why Paul is speaking the way he is.

Do you see how this can illuminate your reading? Find out the context of the book. How old was the person when they wrote it? Where were they geographically? What had they just been doing? Where were they currently going? To whom were they writing? Can you relate to them? Ask any questions that will inform you about how they feel.

We use this strategy to experience the words more and to reveal sometimes hidden information. When you know what the book author's intention was and who they were writing to, an intimate insight into the depth of God's heart is there for the taking.

Chapter Five
Study your calling

What is the difference between pursuing a dream and pursuing a goal? The difference is that a goal can be pursued at any time, while a dream is pursued at the right time, an appointed time, a time not set by you, a time when you are called to realise it.

A Godly dream is like a spiritual deposit. It might be something you have intuitively known about for years, but you know it's just not the right time yet. But having it deposited inside you, can intuitively inform the decisions you make in life. The dream might not be something you can do at just any moment, but if you know it's there, you can prepare for it.

Miraculous confidence

In 1 Samuel 16, God called Samuel the prophet to go to a man in Bethlehem called Jesse so that he could anoint one of his sons as the next king of Israel, the one who was after God's own heart. When Samuel arrived, seven of Jesse's sons passed before him and God instructed Samuel that none of them was to be king. But there was one more son, so Samuel sent for him. Here's verse 12:

"So he sent for him and had him brought in. He was glowing with health and had a fine appearance and handsome features. Then the Lord said, 'Rise and anoint him; this is the one'" 1 Samuel 16:12 (NIV)

The chosen son was David. Sometime after this event, the famous story of David and Goliath took place. I think David's anointing before his fight with Goliath is important. When you read this account in 1 Samuel 17 David seems to have an impossible confidence about him when faced with the prospect of fighting Goliath. He had the confidence to sling a stone accurately enough to hit Goliath with it, amidst all the turmoil of that scene.

Now I suspect that one of the main reasons for this, along with experiencing God powerfully in his life when no one was looking (1 Samuel 17:37), was because David had been anointed as the future king of Israel previously. He hadn't yet become king at that point (when Goliath was taunting Israel), so we might consider things from David's perspective.

David knew how big God is, and trusted Him to give him victory over a giant because he had been anointed and he knew the meaning of this anointing. David had cultivated confidence in God as a young man, and so when he *was* called, he had great reason to be confident in the fight against Goliath that day.

After his anointing, it took many years until David became king. What did David do during this time? He faced many tribulations. Goliath was one of the first. David was banished from King Saul's presence, meaning he had to go on the run, hiding in the desert, forced into exile and fighting many battles.

But amongst the difficulties, we see a beautiful demonstration of his faith in God's calling. David trusted God's word and therefore possessed miraculous confidence and perseverance that might seem impossible to us, but actually, there was a reason and logic to it. Through all this, David was being prepared for his calling.

You are called

You are called into something. As a believer, by default, you are called, did you know that? Have you considered preparing for this by the way you read scripture? Where there is a call from God, there should be faith. Where there is a promise from God, faith is our mode of transport. David's faith in God's promise pulled him through trials that prepared him for his life as king. And by having an attitude of faith he expected God to do something - this expectation overpowered his fear.

For faith to exist there needs to be a promise. Any faith we have as Christians needs to be based on a promise. This is the difference from having faith that you are going to win the lottery when God has not shown you in any way that He is at the end of such a hope, you can't just make up your own faith for anything you like. All Christian faith has to have a promise from God at the base of it. Hebrews 11:1 is the most concise definition of faith in the Bible.

"Now faith is confidence in what we hope for and assurance about what we do not see." Hebrews 11:1 (NIV)

This confidence and assurance are based on promises set by God. So we have faith that these things are true and will happen. We live our lives based on His word. We make our decisions in life based on what He has said and blessing is always at the other end of the promise. There you have the pattern, God speaks through His word and by faith those who love and believe Him pursue this, blessing in some form or another comes along the way.

God's word, His promises, they are precious. They are more reliable and trustworthy than anything else. They are more valuable than any amount of money. All believers are rich because of His promises, do you realise that? When you believe in Him, when you look at His promises, you believe them also. Living in the full reality that Jesus did all that the Bible says is the highest level of revelation possible. All other revelation is merely a slide show compared to this.

But if all real faith needs God to be at the base of it, what about when you feel God is speaking into a situation in your life and it's not something recorded in the Bible? I mentioned before that you cannot just make up your own faith. You cannot set the parameters yourself and say that because you want a certain thing in life, maybe a particular house or a certain partner, and just believe that God will give it to you without this being within His will. Christian faith is not to be confused with the law of attraction where people supposedly believe the things they want into existence.

You cannot just manufacture faith - even faith the size of a mustard seed - and believe for everything you want this way. This means that you can't take a verse like **"Everything is possible for one who believes." Mark 9:23 (NIV)** and then apply it to whatever you like. So we need to apply verses like this in the context of what the Bible says as a whole.

In 1 John 5 it says **"This is the confidence which we have before Him, that, if we ask anything according to His will, He hears us." 1 John 5:14 (NASB).** This means that whatever you ask for needs to correspond to His will. And entering into this verse is based on 1 Samuel 13:14 (NASB) when it talks about how the **"Lord has sought out for Himself a man after His own heart"**, speaking of David. David never got to read the verse in 1 John 5:14, but his life demonstrated that he understood its meaning.

Faith is always built on the foundation of what God has said. And I believe that reading about Him every day in the Bible is one of the most powerful things you can do to learn about who He is, including the parts of scripture that people often overlook. So the point is, when you learn about Him by reading about Him, you get to know Him more and put yourself in a better position to understand what He has said.

'So then, we must cling in faith to all we know to be true' Hebrews 4:14 (TPT)

By faith, we trust God to construct a future for us which is better than the one we make for ourselves. Our faith in God enables us to trust Him for this future, so we must cling to it.

Study your calling

God can call us into many things in life. If you follow Jesus and you're still alive, then you know He has something for you. Is there a certain topic in the Bible that you feel called to understand? Maybe you have a specific calling in life, and reading the Bible with that in mind is going to help you understand it more.

Maybe you feel drawn to the prophetic. Maybe you want to learn about your identity in God, and so learning about His promises from Genesis to Revelation may be the first thing to do to flesh out your kingdom personality. Maybe you want to major in the topic of grace. Or maybe there's a specific thing God is calling you to do, and now you need to prepare for this by studying that topic in the scriptures.

It's about sowing through study in the area of your calling or dream, sowing in the Spirit in faith for a bountiful harvest. Could it be that God is calling you to come out of a trauma from your past that is suppressing your freedom and joy every day? And that He needs you fit for a future calling? What topics in the Bible intrigue and excite you more than anything else? Have you considered that this might be part of the process for preparing for your calling? Even if you are not clear on exactly what your calling might be.

I'm talking about big topics here, things you want to get and understand, things you can build into yourself so that in time they start to show themselves in your character. This can be utterly life-changing.

Look for your calling in scripture

Sometimes I love looking for one thing in the chapters I read because it can get complicated right? Reading scripture, using all these various strategies, sometimes it's quite nice to just read and look for that one thing. Maybe you could start by drawing a line under any verse that appeals and then look at the circumstances surrounding that topic.

Maybe you feel drawn to the gift of healing, and so you comb the whole Bible for situations where healing takes place. You study the surrounding context to see if you can spot any trends that always seem to be there when someone is healed. You will be amazed by how God can change you through this, each day searching for more on that one topic, conditioning and reshaping your mind in that area over months, even years.

The Bible is so layered. Each chapter has so much depth and how far you can go with it seems to be endless. It can be a bit overwhelming sometimes. So a great way to focus on what God is calling you to do is to concentrate on that single topic.

Stepping outside into any street you will see that there are layers upon layers of things to notice, and the layers you take notice of are determined by the way you look at life. You might be a chiropractor and look at the world from this perspective, which means that in the street, you will notice peoples' posture and how it affects the way they walk. You spend so much of your day fixing peoples' backs that's just how you see the world, that's the layer of information you perceive in the street.

Or you might be a car mechanic so you're looking at all the cars, the make, the condition they're in. You might work for the council and therefore you're aware of the bumps in the road, looking for ways to improve the road surface. We all notice different things. The life you live determines the way you see the world, there's almost an endless number of layers you can be aware of just by walking down the street.

The same is true with the Bible. There are so many layers within the chapters that sometimes I find it helpful to look for one specific layer or topic. Maybe there's a certain layer you're looking for, a certain topic that you want to focus on, and this will likely be linked with your calling. That's the layer you want to look for and you ignore everything else. It's fine to do that because sometimes we're called to learn certain topics at certain times.

I find that when people do this, i.e. search for the topic they feel called to study, they then have to read everything else in the Bible anyway in order to find it, so they end up learning many other things they didn't expect. You can of course choose the books that are more specific to your calling, but depending on the topic, sometimes it's more powerful to just read the whole Bible front to back searching for that one thing. Keep your calling in mind the whole time while reading, searching it out, thereby giving God the leverage to really shape the way you think about it. He can then help you see your calling in the street every day – it will become a natural way of thinking.

Maybe you don't know what you're called to do, but you might still have a particularly strong interest in a certain topic in the Bible. If you do, then consider that this might be linked to your calling. Consider that it may be linked to something in your future and this is the faith trail you need to follow. Sometimes it's just best to start with what we're interested in without getting overly spiritual about it.

There again, you might think you have a calling for a certain thing, but then you spend some time reading scripture looking through this lens, and realise that it's not your call. Somehow, however, it relates to it, and therefore the time you've spent reading has begun to refine the purpose you truly hold in your heart. I also think our callings can be like going up mountains sometimes, you approach the top and then you realise there is another hill after that. So we understand that there are dreams beyond dreams.

Goals can function in such a way that they prepare you for your dreams. I'm saying this because not everyone is aware of their dreams, or their calling. If that is you, is it time for you to find out? Life goals can be the very things that activate your dreams.

Are you serving in church? Or considering it? Or having a break from serving and thinking about what's next? Consider that if you don't know of a role that screams out to you, doing the next best thing might be the right thing, as this might inspire you to become aware of your calling. Serving in your local church is such a powerful way for you to shine a light on the work God has for you.

Maybe instead you do know your dream, but you are scared to admit it. What can bring you out of this fear? If there is a light by which you can pursue, a particular direction, a calling you can study in the Bible, this might be the progressive way by which you bring your dream closer to the surface.

I'm talking about purposefully choosing a topic to study in the Bible over a longer period of time, with the intention of this topic manifesting itself through you. It manifests through you because you've studied it and lived with it for so long, six months or several years. This is the kind of length of time and depth of knowledge that will bring about a real progression in your life as a Christian.

Our minds can be highly adaptable as children of God if we train them to be. This is more effective when you spend more time on it, at least a few months, for it to really shape your thinking. When your thinking is shaped around this topic, it's got no choice but to work itself out of you afterwards.

Our bodies are very adaptable and you can exercise physically in a way that will prepare you for certain things. You exercise in a particular way if you play rugby, you would use a different approach if you were training to be a long-distance runner. Over time your body adapts, becomes appropriately built for that task and also ends up looking a certain way. This means the decisions you have made manifest themselves through your appearance and preparedness for the activity you've trained for.

The faith exchange

So how could the man ever be strong enough to carry the bull? Remember the story from the introduction?

The old story was about a man who wanted to get strong, strong enough to carry a bull. His tactic for this was to begin by carrying a calf around his shoulders - walk from his village to another - and back home again once every day. The logic was that because the calf was getting heavier at such a slow pace every day, he thought this would be slow enough for his body to adapt and get stronger alongside it until eventually, the calf grew into the size of a bull which he could then carry.

But the problem with a linear tactic like this, of simply just walking back and forth from village to village each day with the calf around his shoulders, was not enough for the man to grow this strong. Why? Because human bodies eventually stop getting stronger when the same kind of repetitive stimulus is applied over and over again, they stop adapting.

So then how? What strategy could he have used to somehow carry the bull?

The answer is: in the same way that David did the impossible by slaying Goliath. He did that based on the strength that he received through his faith in God's promise. Anytime faith is pursued, there is always an exchange.

By living in faith in God's calling for you, you become empowered by Him because he always provides support when you live like this. Faith always replenishes, giving you the strength to carry things in life that would otherwise be impossible without God.

When walking God's faith-filled journey, He will always provide the perfect stimulus strategy for you to grow continually, getting stronger in life and doing things that would otherwise be impossible.

You were confident as a child playing in the sea and diving into the waves because you knew that if you got swept under the water, your parents would pick you up, they became your strength. God's people can have confidence because their trust is based on what God has said to them, and as a result, He becomes their strength (Exodus 15:2).

Hebrews 11 talks about faith and its rewards. The first part of the verse in Hebrews 11:6 (NIV) says **"And without faith it is impossible to please God"**. In the whole chapter of Hebrews 11, the writer is talking about all the heroes of the Old Testament and how they came to God on the basis of faith. The second part of verse 6 is interesting, it says **"because anyone who comes to him must believe that he exists and that he rewards those who earnestly seek him"**. This verse covers two main points.

Point 1, we can only please God through faith, and point 2, there's an exchange that takes place when we do that. This entire chapter in Hebrews 11 uses the pattern of verse 6 to describe the famous acts of the saints of the Old Testament who sowed and reaped rewards. It talks about an act of faith they had and then the exchange that came from it. There is always an exchange with God when you approach Him on the basis of faith.

Study your calling in the Bible, while trusting *Him* to carry the impossible weight that life can bring to you. The bull in the story is your impossibilities, your mountains, your dreams that you stopped dreaming, or dreams you didn't even know were there because the world suppressed them. It's Jesus that carries the bull, not you. Study your calling by faith my friend.

Defining your Bible reading strategy

Have you considered a personal Bible reading strategy? Maybe you're just starting and you just want to get a feel for it, in which case it might not be that complicated. Maybe you could read the New Testament once through, a little every day. Maybe you could set up some parameters such as reading two chapters a day, starting with Matthew, then you could read all the way to the book of Revelation. Or perhaps read a different Gospel every time you finish a couple of the smaller books.

Maybe you've been reading the Bible for years now and it's become a bit of a chore. Spend some time, maybe a few weeks, considering what the Holy Spirit is saying to you on this. Where do you go from here? Where is the point of faith by which you can move forwards?

Wherever you're at with your Bible reading, it is wise to have a long term strategy. One might say *'I just prefer to see where the spirit takes me'* and yes I agree, but the spirit may be leading you into a specific plan also. Having a long term plan gives focus and intentionality.

Set-up parameters to define your study

I once did a study where I was searching for Jesus in the Old Testament. I felt called to this for several years but didn't know how to go about it. I tried many different things and eventually, I developed a set of key parameters to go by.

I read each chapter in the Old Testament several times until I could highlight a given thing that stood out to me. And then I asked a simple question *"what's the relationship between that thing and Jesus? How do they link up?"* and then like magic, just from that simple question, I started to find Him everywhere in the Old Testament. I did around a chapter a day, every day, and recorded voice memos for my notes.

Study your calling

These were the parameters or rules that I used to define my study, simple but extremely deep. And the more parameters you set, the more specific the study becomes.

If you want to join a gym and your goal is to get fit, that is a very broad parameter, almost too broad. It means you are left with too many options as to what you do when you exercise. The phrase *'the person who chases two rabbits, catches neither'* comes to mind. But having said that, I do acknowledge that maybe you need a simple goal such as 'getting fit' to begin with, such as reading the whole Bible once through to get a general feel for it. Your reading can become more specific as you go.

It took me about a year and a half of doing this study every day, and I can tell you that the person I started the study as was different to the person who finished it, no exaggeration. If I'd only done it for say three months, I don't think it would have affected me as much because it wouldn't have been long enough. So it required a longer period of time for these truths to really permeate me.

If you can figure out a set of parameters, boundaries to stay within for your study, spend a week or two testing them out over some scripture before you begin, refining your rules as you go. If you come up with something that feels right, write it down and memorise the structure of your study so each time you sit down to read, you know exactly what to do. That's your plan.

Now at this time did I have a specific understanding of a future call from God? Well, I was vague about it. I wasn't necessarily clear, however, I knew this was the study I wanted to do. God's calling to us can very much work like building blocks. One call takes you a brick higher, and as you get closer to the top, you can start to see things above you more clearly. You also gain a greater bird's eye view of things below you, meaning you can help those who are yet to know their calling.

Ask a well thought out question to reveal a revelation

Maybe you could do a study on God's heart, on His perspective, the objective being to align your heart more to his, maybe you're specifically called to something like this? I think David did this study. You study what God wants, His heart, His perspective throughout the Bible. And to do this you might need to ask some questions to open things up.

Any time God does something in the Bible, anything that you can see, start by asking 'why?'. Do this in a way that's manageable for you. If you have five questions to ask every time you see the topic you're looking for, this might be too much. But if you keep it simple and ask one well thought out question, you could simply ask *"why did God do that?"*. Ask that same question every time you get to a place in the Bible where God does something, which of course is a lot of places and can be done across the whole Bible. Or every time you see God asking a question in the Bible, stop to understand why. Similarly, every time people ask God questions in the Bible, consider why they were asking.

Test something out, trial a question to see if it unlocks the layer of revelation you're looking for, if it doesn't work, re-word the question. Every time I begin a new study plan, it tends to need a month or two of trial and error until it starts to click.

If you can figure out how to catch your own fish here, rather than always relying on someone else to catch it for you, relying on someone else to find the revelations in the Bible, then the speed at which you'll grow will be so much faster. If you did this study, to learn God's heart and perspective on things, that can change your world, what would happen from there? Perhaps you would start to think more like God and have the same concerns as Him.

The right questions stimulate the right answers

Maybe you want to do a study on women role models in the Bible. But not just the obvious women, and so you go a little further and read all the books in the Bible searching for women that you admire. That's a study for men to do too - not just for the women by the way. Any men reading this? Be open to a calling that produces or supports women leaders in the church in some way.

When you find these women in the Bible, what then? What do you do? Do you just read about them and move on? Or do you want to look for something specific? You could ask a simple question *"what is the relationship between that particular woman and Jesus?"* And then this might open up the revelation. But if that doesn't work, try a different question such as - *"how did God use that woman?"* or *"What did the woman do to serve God?"*. When you ask the right questions they start to inspire the right information. This begins the process of bringing the revelation *closer*.

Have you ever been in a conversation when someone has asked you questions that don't inspire you? And your answers end up being a little plain or flat. But then some people, who are really skilled and know how to stimulate great conversations by asking the right questions, the experience is transformed. It's the same idea here with studying your calling. You find the subject you're called to learn about, and then ask the right questions that inspire the revelation. This might take a bit of experimentation and prodding.

'Method act' your calling in the Bible

Maybe your heart longs for being prophetic, and so you search for all prophetic situations in the Bible and create a plan on how you're going to read them. Now you could search the internet for all these passages in isolation, but if the subject is consistent enough in the Bible, I think there's something powerful about making the effort yourself. It means you have to almost get into the mindset of the character or theme every time you read the Bible, giving God better leverage to reshape how you see things in life.

Take the example of the 'method' actor. Before being on camera, they spend time getting into the mindset and attitude of the character they are playing beforehand, so that when the camera is rolling, they're not so much acting anymore, but showing reality. And it is often been said that these actors remain in character even when the camera stops filming because they are so used to it by that point. How much more will this work for you when you are acting out a truth that is for you to embrace?

Put on the glasses through which you see that topic each time you sit down to read the Bible. Over time, you will inevitably think about that topic more, this will lead you to view the world through these changed lenses, and you'll start to see this theme when you walk down the street.

Maybe each time you find a prophetic passage, you look at its context. You look at the time the prophecy was given and then you search for its fulfilment. Then maybe after that, you could try to figure out why the prophecy had to be fulfilled when it did, to understand God's plan. As much as I enjoy reading scripture without a plan and just seeing where it takes me, my growth is great and more specific to my call when I have parameters to go by. How about you?

Search the scriptures through the lens of your calling, and then God can awaken a gift in you. Now sure enough I could lay out a generic study for you and write out exactly what you are to do, what you are to read, the questions you should ask. But it will never be specific to you personally. So I encourage you my friend, to be open to the Holy Spirit helping you to create your own Bible study, let Him show you how to do it.

Dress for the role you want in life before you do it

Are you feeling a sense that you would like to be a preacher, or be involved in ministry? So you decide to read every chapter in the Bible, then ask a simple question in each chapter such as *"How do I preach the gospel from this chapter?"* - You do that every day, going through every chapter for a couple of years, even the chapters you find difficult. Think about how that can change you. It's a long enough period to shape your mind into a certain way and prepare you for the role you want in life before you do it. They say that *'luck is when preparation meets opportunity'*. Use the Bible to prepare you for opportunities that turn into your dreams.

To summarise

I have given some examples which may or may not do anything for you. Sometimes when you don't know what to do, it's good to just do something anyway. Do the next best thing that you desire even if it doesn't scream out to you, follow the trail and see where it takes you.

The main point that all my Bible study examples here illustrate, is that you're looking for one thing in scripture. One topic that is either directly or indirectly to do with your calling. I say indirectly because even if you do not know what you are called for, God so often leads us along a trail of faith-driven activities that prepare and lead us to the things that truly satisfy our hearts. And when you look back at that trail of faith you followed, you see a harvest a hundred times more than which was sown.

So what subject do you want to see in the Bible? What do you feel called for? Maybe your Bible reading has become flat and it's time to just look for one specific thing. What are the top three things you want to know about God? Choose the first thing, and figure out a way to study it by asking the right questions that will inspire the right information. What you are doing here is creating your own personalised Bible study, taking control. Don't always leave it up to someone else to create your study.

God designed faith in such a way that there is always an exchange that takes place when we live by it. It has built within it a replenishment cycle. When walking in faith in God and His promises, we live our lives so that our decisions are informed by what we have faith for. In the time from doing this, our life starts to form the shape of what we have faith for, and this reshaped life better supports us in our calling. Christian faith always requires God's word at the end of it as a target to aim for, and it always replenishes and blesses us when pursued. Not only do we see this in King David's life, but the lives of many others in the Bible (as seen in Hebrews 11).

The purpose for doing this is so you can become and embody the topic that you feel called to learn about. When you do this for long periods, it starts to become you. Find a way to learn about your calling in the Bible, and over time you will start to embody that calling - seeing it all over the place.

Chapter Six

Emotional simulation

Every room that has people inside it will have a certain emotional feel. For example, a staff room - imagine you're there on your own. You're likely to feel a certain way, thinking about your own day and your own circumstances while having a break.

Let's continue with this example. Let's say:

You started work at 9am and it's your first break at 12pm. You've been sitting in your staff room for around ten minutes and you're feeling quite relaxed. But then a manager walks in. You immediately feel a slight tension, you aren't quite as relaxed as you were before, purely because he or she is there now.

So the manager sits near you, you're chatting away with him/her. You don't have a particular problem with them, but you don't consider them as your friend either. You're engaging in small talk that you'd probably prefer not to on your break. Five minutes pass, and then one of your co-worker friends comes in. As soon as you see her walk into the room you immediately

Emotional simulation

feel a sense of relief. You are comfortable around her, and her being there divides the slight awkwardness you had with your manager. She sits next to you both, and the manager starts to have the same conversation with her as with you. Now you go back to feeling a bit more like you did when you were sitting on your own, with a mild sense of relief, not quite the same as before but similar.

A powerful technique to use when reading the Bible is *Emotional Simulation*. This is when you put yourself in the shoes of the people you're reading about in order to simulate what they were feeling, and doing this with all character types, including the enemies.

Now when I explained this staff room story did you feel anything? Could you relate to it? You might have been in a similar situation before. If not you have likely experienced enough situations in life to be able to accurately imagine this one. It's not the wildest story in the world but it's a common kind of situation that happens every day. And just thinking about it enables you to emotionally manufacture a very distinct and specific feeling. What if I told the same story, but condensed it like this instead:

You had a break in your staff room, your manager walked in and you spoke to each other, and then your friend came in and she spoke to your manager.

I'm describing the same event but without any emotional references. Often, the Bible does the same. So we need an emotional awareness, or contextual understanding of the characters to fill in what happens with emotion. The Bible is full of scenarios with emotional dynamics we might not be aware of and it's very easy to miss out on these things unless you're actively thinking about them.

To simulate the emotions attached to people's experiences in the Bible, to understand the emotional atmosphere of the setting, a really powerful thing to do is to think of a scenario in your life that most closely resembles the scene that you're reading about. This will enable you to relate to it. If you think about it, it doesn't matter if it was 2000 or 5000 years ago, we experience the same emotions today.

Example one – The prophet without honour

In Mark 6:1-6, there's the story of *the prophet without honour* when Jesus came back to his home town in Nazareth to teach. Until Jesus began His ministry, His deity was hidden, so all the townsfolk had no idea who He really was as He was growing up. And now, all of a sudden, they're seeing a side to Him they've never seen before. They start asking all these sceptical questions about Him because He's teaching with this great authority. The townsfolk are asking *'where did all this come from?'*, *'we know this guy'*, and probably *'who does He think he is? He was never like that before'*.

In this scene, there are three main character groups. You have the townsfolk who are saying all these sceptical things about Jesus, that's one. Then you have Jesus' disciples, that's two. And then Jesus Himself, that's the third. I want to talk about what each of these groups were experiencing.

Character one – The townsfolk

Let's start with the townsfolk. How do they feel when they see

Jesus doing all these great things? So our question is *'well how would I feel about that?'*

Have you ever been in a workplace where one of your colleagues, who started at the company at the same time as you, with a similar level of experience, gets a promotion before you do? Not through any bad practice, they deserve it - and they get more money, more responsibility and their own team to lead.

Have you ever experienced a situation like this or have an idea of the emotion involved? You are going to be left behind by that person, and now you feel a sense of resentment towards them. You're jealous and thinking *'who does he think he is? Look at him, he thinks he's so good'*. Have you ever felt like that before? It's nothing that the promoted person has done, the problem is in your attitude, this really ugly attitude. And I think, even though this is a different kind of scenario to the scene in Mark 6, I think these emotions may be similar to what the townsfolk would have felt.

Simulating the emotion here is possible because two people can experience the same or similar emotions in different scenarios. You might not have ordered someone's death as David did to Uriah the Hittite, but you might have made a mistake in your life where you tried to cover it up, instead of doing the right thing. So you know what it's like for your face to feel heated when doing the wrong thing - you know what it feels like when your breathing becomes more intense just at that moment. Because if you've done something like that, even if it wasn't at the same magnitude as David wrongfully taking someone's life, you can still amplify the emotion you have felt to simulate the bigger scale of this scene.

Character two – The disciples

Character group two is the disciples. How might they have felt in this scene? They seem to be right in the middle of it, twelve of them following Jesus, hanging on to every word He says. They don't always understand Him and are always playing catch up with His teachings, but they trust Him. How would they have felt here?

Well, the townsfolk took offence at Jesus. It's possible that the disciples may have felt offended themselves by this when they knew how much integrity Jesus has. A feeling of anger and offence towards the townsfolk and a feeling of being protective about Jesus. There may have been some slight measure of awkwardness for them also. So perhaps they were experiencing a mixture of being offended, feeling protective, and to a degree, awkward. It's difficult to simulate and feel this mix of emotions unless we think about this scene from their perspective, in a first-person mode, so we have to pause and imagine it.

This scene in the Bible might give you enough on its own to simulate the emotions present, but to bring it a little closer to home we can go back to the office scene. That's the same office scene as before but from somebody else's perspective. This time you're another character.

You're a new recruit in this company, fresh out of university, and the person who just got promoted is now your boss. You look up to them, they're someone you want to be like, someone who will influence you. And then all of a sudden you see your boss's old co-worker walking past, making sneering comments under their breath about them. You might feel a sense of being protective about your boss and a bit angry towards your boss's old co-worker for saying these things. But it's a specific type of anger - offence. Mixed in with this are feelings of confusion and also injustice. You'd maybe want to step in and say something to protect your boss. But this might be a bit above your pay grade so you just keep quiet and observe. That's how I think the disciples felt here in this passage.

A quick note - comparing the imagined office events to the Bible story might seem to take a while to consider and thus risk breaking up the flow of your Bible reading session. But really, considering this can take only seconds when you understand the context of the setting. The point is that it won't take long to consider these emotions and there won't be any risk of draining your energy in your reading session.

Character three – Jesus

Lastly, character three, the perspective of Jesus. So before we start to think like a human here, and think about our own perspective, we have to consider that this is the perspective from God Himself, Jesus - the perspective of perfect love.

We have to be aware that everything Jesus ever did or said was always, always, always driven by love. We have to look at this from the perspective that Jesus was fully man and fully God and that He was without sin. That's how you need to approach Jesus' perspective all the time.

Okay, so let's get into His shoes as best as we can. Imagine being the person who got promoted in this office scene, and how you would feel if you knew that your old co-worker, with whom you always got on well, was gossiping about you and resenting you because of your promotion. How would that make you feel?

You would probably feel a slight sense of being stabbed in the back or betrayed or deceived. You would feel like the relationship was perhaps over but finished on their terms, not yours.

But, if all your actions are being driven by love (as in Jesus' case), mixed into this feeling of being stabbed in the back, you would be feeling a sense of hurt and pain. Maybe a slightly sour taste in your mouth. This was a co-worker you were friends with, perhaps you even loved them as a friend.

These are the main emotional elements here. You had love for this person, but they stabbed you in the back. This combination of feelings produces pain. It hurts to know that this happened. So what do you do? The co-worker has shut themselves off to you. What can you do? It's sad to say, but the best thing you can do (for now) is to just leave them alone.

So we've got three characters. The townsfolk, simulated in the bitter co-worker who's jealous because he's been left behind – it was another person who got promoted. Then the disciples, simulated in the new recruit who is protective over their boss and angry about the co-worker's attitude. And lastly, Jesus, simulated in the one who got promoted, who feels hurt and stabbed in the back by someone he loves.

At the start of this chapter, we imagined three people in the staff room. When there was only one person, the room felt a certain way. When there were two people, the feel changed significantly. When there were three, it changed yet again. With three people in the room, the three vibes combined to produce a complex, group effect. This seems complicated to describe as a whole, but easier to understand when you view it from each person's individual perspective.

Emotional simulation

So, in the prophet without honour passage, where we've explored each of the three character group's feelings in isolation, there is another vibe - the combination of the three groups. And why is this important to consider? I believe that Jesus was aware of this. Having the highest emotional intelligence possible teaches us about God's heart. It teaches us about what Jesus was experiencing and what He felt. What a beautiful thing.

Before moving on to the next example, let's read the actual biblical account carefully. See how you feel. It might be overwhelming now when considering the depth of the feelings involved. Perhaps read it thinking of only one of the character groups, or consider the overall feel from the heart of God.

"Jesus went out from there and came into His hometown; and His disciples followed Him. When the Sabbath came, He began to teach in the synagogue; and the many listeners were astonished, saying, "Where did this man get these things, and what is this wisdom given to Him, and such miracles as these performed by His hands? Is not this the carpenter, the son of Mary, and brother of James and Joses and Judas and Simon? Are not His sisters here with us?" And they took offence at Him. Jesus said to them, "A prophet is not without honour except in his hometown and among his own relatives and in his own household." And He could do no miracles there except that He laid His hands on a few sick people

and healed them. And He wondered at their unbelief." Mark 6:1-6 (NASB)

Now you don't have to replicate the exact same emotions when using this strategy, but you are looking to get the closest match – to simulate. So there needs to be a level of wisdom here so that you're not turning a scene into something different. If you don't know how to simulate the emotion then you might need to gain a better understanding of the passage first.

Emotional simulation helps you to experience what you're reading, which is a better way in terms of self-teaching than being emotionally distant from the scene. It has a powerful effect on you to be a 'doer', and an active participating agent in the word, not just a spectator.

Example two – David & Bathsheba

Here's another example: David watching Bathsheba bathing in 2 Samuel 11. He took her for himself that night, even though she was married to another man. You know, I think seeing her naked would have been an extremely intense moment for him. She was very beautiful, and David with the power he had, knew he could have her. He knew he was doing something wrong, but he did it quickly, so he would have less time to dwell on it.

The man famous for being after God's own heart, in this scene, turned a blind eye to God's heart, listening to the devil's worldly way of living for the moment. And through this, the devil would yet again attempt to bring an end to the family that Jesus would come from. An extremely intense lustful moment.

Have you ever felt something like that? Tempted to do something you really should not have done, and doing it quickly in an attempt to bypass the feeling of guilt (even though you know you won't escape this in the end), because of how good it feels in the moment of wrong doing. How did it make you feel? There's an intensity to it, something sinister in it. You're feeling hot in your chest. But it also feels good, a spoiled, rotten form of goodness.

What about Bathsheba? What do we know about her that tells us about how she felt day to day and in this situation? She is beautiful, this would make her feel a certain way each and every day, getting more attention than most women. She was married to Uriah, so it is likely that her husband is regularly in her thoughts. At this point he is away fighting in a war, thus affecting the way she's feeling about the future. She was washing from her monthly period as required by the law in a place where she could be seen (her roof) by David.

God's perspective? He saw and understood it all. What does this teach us? Many things, potentially. We are reminded that God sees everything. There are more characters in this story, such as Uriah, Joab and Nathan the prophet. You could take the emotional simulation technique quite far here, simulating each person's feelings. It's a very powerful tool to use - but should be approached wisely.

Sometimes movie directors give their actors information about the characters they are playing that we as the audience don't get to know about. And they do this so the actor can add more detail and depth to their acting, based on this undisclosed back story. Because of this, they can feel what that character is supposed to be feeling, which enables them to act a certain way.

We can be the method actors in these scenes in scripture, in that we can explore the backstories of the characters. But it's not just the backstories we get, but the future story also, because we know what happens after the events we're reading about. We're then able to link the emotions from the current reading to future situations. This means, we can understand some of what they felt at the time, but we can also access God's perspective and heart because He knew what would happen in the future. And that's the powerful thing - insight into God's heart, because He also knew the before and after as well as the 'during' of the scene that was happening.

It is up to you how far you take this strategy - and indeed any other in this book for that matter. Pick and mix from the various strategies as you please, the Holy Spirit will show you what to do, just keep your heart and mind open to Him. You don't have to use a strategy for every character in the scene you're reading, just for the ones you can and the ones you want to. I know there are a lot of words describing these strategies, but it only really takes seconds to think about it and put it into practice when you understand what's going on.

Example three – Peter's denial of Jesus

Simulating the emotions of the people in the Bible is a wonderful way to feel the Bible. And each example I have given didn't take a lot of thought to find because this is a strategy we can use all over the Bible. In this last example, I want to talk about Peter's denial of Jesus.

Shortly before Jesus is arrested and crucified, He prophesies to His disciple Peter and says **"before the rooster crows, you will disown me three times"** Matthew 26:34 (NIV).

Shortly after this happens, Peter is approached by three different people who say *"aren't you the guy that was with Jesus?"* And because Peter is so scared of being found out and persecuted for being associated with Jesus, who is currently on trial, he responds in the heat of the moment and says **"I don't know the man!"** So what is going on here?

It is interesting because Jesus said this to Peter shortly before Peter denied Him. So you would think that Peter would have had His words at the forefront of his mind and he would *definitely not* have disowned Jesus in that situation -especially because he then swore to Jesus that he would never do this.

Immediately after Peter said **"I don't know the man!"** a rooster crowed. At that moment, Peter remembered what Jesus had said, and he went outside and wept bitterly. Isn't it interesting how intense emotions and the power of self-interest can make us forget what we are supposed to do?

This failure in Peter's life had such a profound effect on him that around thirty years later he would go on to write what we now call 1 Peter - a letter written to encourage believers who were being persecuted for following Jesus. Do you see the connection?

He wanted to support people in the area in which he failed - denying Jesus to avoid persecution. This failure was something that had such an effect on Peter that it stayed with him for all these years. It partly shaped his life for the better, because he loved God. Humans instinctively want restoration from sin, oh how beautiful that God can use this instinct for His glory! Jesus knew this as we see when He restored Peter (John 21:15-17).

How do you think Peter would have felt when he realised what he had done? Have you ever been caught red-handed doing something you knew you shouldn't, and then, just at the moment you were caught, your eyes suddenly opened and you thought *"what have I done?!"*

For example - you were taking too many breaks at work and the manager told you to stop. But you didn't take the warning seriously enough. They caught you at it again but this time they flipped out, and then suddenly your eyes were opened. So this experience of being caught taught you something - you knew you would never do it again, and learned to become a model of integrity.

You were somehow blinded before. When you repeat the same sin, you start to get used to it. You start to find false ways to justify yourself and start to think it's not such a big deal anymore, becoming blind in the process. Sin always finds you out. How did you feel when you were caught? Maybe your face went red, maybe you started to feel hot around your face and chest, maybe you were starting to get a little sweaty? You were caught red-handed, and you had to explain yourself.

I think this is partly how Peter felt when the rooster crowed, coupled with guilt but at a much deeper level than the example I just gave of a situation at work. Peter seemed to be a confident guy so what a humbling experience this must have been for him. Can you feel the intensity of this moment? I get that not everyone will stop to simulate these feelings when reading verses. But if you stop to think about a situation you have been in like this, you feel it, at least in a distant way.

To summarise

Now this is something you can do in so many places in the Bible - role-playing characters if you have enough information about them. Use this whenever you feel it's the right time to use it. I think it works as a wonderful way to feel scripture. The effect it has on you can really bring you closer to God.

You are wise to learn from your own mistakes in life, but you are even wiser to learn from the mistakes of others. This strategy, my friend, is a powerful way to help you experience that. Being close to God allows you to learn from what He has put in the Bible so that you can experience the successes and failures of people alongside them. You can genuinely learn from them because you can walk their stories with them.

Search to feel the emotions in the Bible, because when you do that, you start to get closer to the perspective of God. It turns the Bible into this amazing, more than 3D experience and shows you a richness you may not have considered before.

Chapter Seven
Looking for the bigger picture

You might remember a television series that came out years ago called *'Lost'*. It was a story about a group of people on a plane that crash-landed on a desert island. They had to learn how to survive and make a life for themselves. There were lots of plot twists and confusing storylines.

It's been said that the bigger picture was that it was a reflection of the many people in the world who were very lost in their lives. I watched the whole series as a teenager but I didn't see the bigger picture theme that it was supposedly communicating, I only realised that years later. When I thought back to the time I was watching it, I was thinking, *'wow, that was speaking to me'* because I was as lost as lost can get in life at that time.

One of the most valuable lessons I learned from Bible college years ago, was to always look for the bigger picture in the Bible story you're reading. You have the up-close meaning - what it's saying there and then at that moment - but you also have the 'zoomed out' message that God, through the writers, often intends you to see.

Example one – The fall of Jericho

God is so powerful that He guides things to happen in real life in such a way that events form parts of a bigger story visible from a different perspective. I'm going to give you an example in scripture of how He interlaces or weaves bigger picture stories into the Bible. Then I want to explain to you why this is important for us, aside from being an interesting way to tell a story. There is a bigger reason.

Have you ever heard of *The fall of Jericho*? It's in the Old Testament in the book of Joshua between chapters 2 and 6. The famous Moses has recently died, and his successor Joshua is now the leader of Israel. The nation is on the cusp of taking the Promised Land, but to do this, they need to take out all the corrupt nations that live there. Before they go in, Joshua sends out two spies to check out the land to see what they're up against. The two spies went to the city of Jericho within the Promised Land and stayed at the house of a prostitute called Rahab.

The King of Jericho found out about the spies and they became wanted men - as you would expect - but this lady Rahab very wisely hid them in her house. She said to the spies that the people of Jericho knew about their nation Israel, they knew that they had defeated all these other nations, and that apparently, Jericho was next on the list. Because of that, the people in Jericho were terrified of the God of Israel.

So when there was news that Israelite spies were checking out Jericho, the people were scared, as they should have been. But Rahab said this to the spies she was hiding:

"Now then, please swear to me by the Lord that you will show kindness to my family, because I have shown kindness to you. Give me a sure sign that you will spare the lives of my father and mother, my brothers and sisters, and all who belong to them – and that you will save us from death" Joshua 2:12-13 (NIV)

And the spies responded with a yes, **'our lives for your lives!'** So she lowered them down out of a window to help them. It just so happened that her house was part of the city wall of Jericho, meaning they were able to escape directly into the land outside. But right before they left, the two spies told her this important detail:

"This oath you made us swear will not be binding on us unless, when we enter the land, you have tied this scarlet cord in the window through which you let us down, and unless you have brought your father and mother, your brothers and all your family into your house. If any of them go outside your house into the street, their blood will be on their own heads; we will not be responsible. As for those who are in the house with you, their blood will be on our head if a hand is laid on them. But if you tell what we are doing, we

will be released from the oath you made us swear." "Agreed," she replied. "Let it be as you say." So she sent them away, and they departed. And she tied the scarlet cord in the window. Joshua 2:17-21 (NIV)

So Rahab agreed. The two spies escaped, went back to their camp and told the Israelite leader Joshua everything. The next morning, the whole Israelite camp marched out on a journey to Jericho.

When they arrived, God asked Joshua to do something peculiar. He asked him to make the Israelite army and priests march around the city of Jericho, carrying the Ark of the Covenant, once a day for six days. On the seventh day, they were to march around it seven times. Then, at that point, the priests of Israel were to blow their trumpets as a signal to the Israelite nation, to give a loud shout and war cry. At that very moment, the walls of Jericho were to fall, not by a bulldozer, but by the hand of God.

Joshua did as God said. The priests carrying the Ark of the Covenant, along with the army, marched around the city of Jericho, once a day for six days. And on the seventh day, they marched around the city wall, how many times? Seven times. The priests blew their trumpets, and then Joshua commanded the army to raise the war cry, just as God had said. Joshua also told the army, to not lay a finger on Rahab and her family (Joshua 6:17) because of the promise that was made, not to touch the house with the *scarlet cord* hanging from the window.

Then the army shouted the war cry. At that point, the walls around the city of Jericho, by a miracle of God, collapsed. Joshua told the two spies from earlier in the story to go to the house of Rahab the prostitute and take her and her family to safety. Her mother, father, brothers and sisters, all in accordance with the oath they had sworn, were taken to safety outside the city. Then, they burned the city down. Rahab and her family lived with the Israelites afterwards.

Now when you look at some artistic images of the fall of Jericho, what you will see are pictures of almost all of the city walls destroyed, but with one lone wall standing high and unscathed, with a scarlet cord hanging out of the window. Rahab and her family were inside, safe and sound. God destroyed the walls but kept Rahab's wall safe because of the oath that was made. This is one of many epic stories in the Old Testament.

The bigger picture

So what I want to do now is show you how to see the bigger picture of what's going on here. I've just told you the in-person story itself, the contextual on the ground story. But what else is it saying to us? Aside from the fact that it's a good bedtime story for children. What does it mean for us today? It's not just there to entertain us like a movie. There's something bigger going on.

I want to teach you a very simple strategy that will allow you to see the bigger picture in every story in the Old Testament. I can sum it up in a sentence, and I really want you to get this because it has the power to unlock so much treasure in the Bible for you.

Have an awareness, that every story in the Old Testament, is a spiritual indicator of what Jesus would eventually do.

How you see the bigger picture in the Old Testament stories is by realising that all the various components in the stories act like props on a stage. Whether it's people, places, or objects, many of these act as what Bible scholars call *'types of Christ'*, things that represent Jesus. The whole of the Bible is one big story about Jesus, including the Old Testament stories.

In the story I've just shared with you, did anything stand out? How do you relate that story to Jesus? Well as a starting point, one of the most significant things in the story is the *scarlet cord*. I just mentioned *'types of Christ'*. This scarlet cord is a type of Christ. Why? Because it represents what would happen later in history when those who follow Jesus are covered and protected by His blood, in the same way, that Rahab and her family were covered and protected by the oath sworn with the spies. The oath worked because of the scarlet cord, representing Jesus's blood.

Also notice in the story how Rahab was referred to as a prostitute (Joshua 2:1). Remember that there are no wasted words in scripture. We don't know why Rehab was a prostitute, but we do know this would have made her an outcast from 'respectable' society. She survived the destruction of her city not because of her righteousness, but because of the oath made with the two spies. This oath points forward to the promise that God made with mankind:

"For God so loved the world, that He gave His only begotten Son, that whoever believes in Him shall not perish, but have eternal life." John 3:16 (NASB).

Our salvation comes not from our own good behaviour or righteousness, but from trusting that the blood of Jesus covers and protects us.

Rahab's survival was not because she was morally better than anyone else, but because an oath had been sworn and kept. Today, those who are followers of Jesus are covered by His blood, like Rehab was covered by the scarlet cord. We're not saved because we're any better than anyone else, we're saved because of a promise. What promise?

The promise is that those who follow Jesus are spiritually covered from eternal separation from God. By the shedding of Jesus' blood, we are saved, we are protected by being inside Him, like Rehab was protected by being inside the walls, not marked for death, but marked for life by the scarlet cord. Go back to the story again in Joshua and notice the difference in what you see.

You can do this with many of the Old Testament stories. God strategically designed history this way. As an artist, He uses our failures and our mistakes for things of powerful significance.

Why is this kind of story-telling important for us today?

At the beginning of the chapter, I said I would explain why this is important for us now, not just because it's interesting to have bigger pictures woven into stories, but because there is a real reason for their ability to empower us today. What's the point in looking for the bigger picture in all these stories?

Quite a few things are useful here. The bigger picture approach teaches us that God somehow managed to weave Jesus into real-life events over and over for centuries. But here's the main point I want to highlight:

When you can see the bigger picture of what God is saying in the individual stories in the Bible, what you see gives you a greater ability to know what God is saying to you in your life. Hear me out here.

Everything that God does has beauty to it. Everything God ever does contains truth, beauty and love. Everything - it's like his signature. Test that out. Think of anything God has done in your life, and tell me it didn't contain truth, beauty and love, among other things. Learning to see these things in scripture shows you how poetic, creative and artistic God is. This then shows you how every act He has done in your life is also filled with His creative beauty.

When we find these things in scripture it has an effect on us. For example - You may read a story in the Bible that you've known about for years, let's say an Old Testament story, and somehow you then realise Jesus is all over that story. How does that affect you? Aside from the fact that it's a revelation to spot these things, it teaches you that Jesus was always there. And do you know what else? I don't think I'm exaggerating here - I think it teaches you to realise that Jesus was always there with you, before you followed Him. Before you formally met him, He was there.

Trace it back, if you can't see Jesus in your life before you followed Him, it's not because He wasn't there, it's because you haven't realised it yet. How do you realise this? Well, one way is to use this strategy. Always looking for the bigger picture in God's word teaches you how to see Him in places you couldn't have acknowledged before, including in your past - before you knew Him.

After I became a Christian, I looked back to the years before I made that decision. I realised that there were things that happened in my past that showed shadows of the cross, certain life experiences. So when the story of Jesus was eventually preached to me, I realised a similarity between my personal experiences from the past, and the Gospel. It's like I was subliminally taught the Gospel before I knew about it with my head.

When you look at the scriptures before Jesus was born, you can see that God does the same thing. He subliminally presents the Gospel to the world, through all these Old Testament stories, like the fall of Jericho. To the point that one day **"when the fullness of time had come" Galatians 4:4 (ESV)** He entered our world not to show us subliminally any-more, not to hire out props such as walls, scarlet cords, actors and actresses to play out the Gospel for us, but to play it Himself, King Jesus, God in the flesh. He came to show us His love in person.

So Jesus's life is in your past, your present and your future. How do I know that? Look at His life. Jesus' life was a retelling of the story of Israel. He went down into the Jordan River - a nod to the crossing of the Red Sea in Exodus. He faced temptation in the wilderness - a nod to Israel's time wandering in the wilderness. He gathered twelve disciples - a nod to the twelve tribes of Israel. He became our intercessor - a nod to Moses speaking to God on behalf of the Israelites. The last supper on the night before His crucifixion is a nod to the Passover meal before the Israelites left Egypt.

His life retells the story of Israel, acknowledging that He was in the bigger picture all along. That means the story of Israel looked forward to Jesus, and Jesus's life looked back to Israel's story. The Old Testament stories look forward to the cross, and all the wisdom in the New Testament looks back to it.

This indicates to us that Jesus was always there in your life before you formally met and followed Him. It tells us that no matter what your life was like before, He was always there. It tells us that no matter what your life is like now, He is here with you, closer than the breath in your lungs. And it tells us that He is in your future, in this life and the next for eternity. You are utterly covered, loved, utterly cradled, utterly surrounded and filled by Him.

How do you see him in the stories?

How do you see the bigger picture in all the Bible stories? You can read them and then think *'okay what's the bigger picture here?'*, but sometimes that gives you a bit too much to think about. Remember that *the right questions inspire the right answers*. So here's a way to do it that might make it a little easier.

Firstly when I say look for the bigger picture in what is going on, it will always be about Jesus - the subject matter of the bigger picture, always. It's as simple as this. Choose a story in the Old Testament, read the story, and ask this question, *'what is the relationship between this story and Jesus?'* And then try to find the link. What things in the story could be *'types'* of Jesus? If you've just started reading the Bible it might be difficult to see this sort of thing at the moment, but knowing this early on can give you an awareness and perception of where He might be when you do read the Old Testament.

You can do this in the New Testament also. But now, you don't need to look for Jesus because by this point He has been revealed. So unlike looking for Jesus in the Old Testament to see the power behind the story, with the New Testament, you are instead using the power of Jesus to make the stories He talks about a reality in your life. But to keep the focus, I will continue to talk about the Old Testament.

Important side note: whenever you think you see Jesus in an Old Testament story, it would be a wise move to compare your findings to what other people say, your pastors, Bible commentaries and so on, to protect yourself from making things up. Over time, through a process of refining and filtering, you will become better at being able to spot Him.

Example two – Other stories

Noah's ark, what is the relationship between this story and Jesus? He's the ark. But how? Look at the story. God is transporting Noah and his family from death to life only by the means of the ark while the world perishes. Inside the ark they are safe. What happens when we follow Jesus? He takes us from death to life while the world perishes. Inside Him we are safe, we cannot swim to survive without Him. Often there are wonderful details to these kinds of stories - such as the wood that was used to build the ark: gopher wood. This was apparently a strong, durable and incorruptible wood. It wasn't going to rot and it wasn't going to be destroyed by insects. This points to the incorruptible nature of Jesus as a sinless man.

But how do you know I'm not just making these things up? My short answer is that when you read the Bible, through and through, you start to see these things all over the place to the point where you can't just call them flukes or coincidences – they're all over the place.

But here is another way to back up what I'm saying. One of the greatest Bible studies that ever happened was shortly after the resurrection of Jesus. Two people were walking on the road to Emmaus, a place that was a seven-mile walk from Jerusalem. These two people were talking about all the things that had just happened with Jesus. And then the resurrected Jesus Himself joined them on the journey, but they couldn't recognise Him. Now, these two people were upset because they had hoped that Jesus was going to be the redeemer of Israel, and they thought that because He died, He wasn't the redeemer. But as they were walking, while He was still unknown to them, Jesus rebuked them and said this:

"How foolish you are, and how slow to believe all that the prophets have spoken! (Prophets in the Old Testament). Did not the Messiah have to suffer these things and then enter his glory?" (As in, He was supposed to die, that wasn't the end). And beginning with Moses and all the Prophets, he explained to them what was said in all the Scriptures concerning himself." Luke 24:25-27 (NIV) (My notes added in brackets).

The greatest Old Testament Bible study ever! I said it was a seven-mile walk, so this study might have been a couple of hours long. Towards the end of the walk, they recognised who He was. Jesus then disappeared, and they said to each other.

"Were not our hearts burning within us while he talked with us on the road and opened the Scriptures to us?" Luke 24:32 (NIV)

That's the word right there, *'burning'*. That's what happens when you find Him, that's what happens when you get revelation like these two people, and your eyes are *'opened'* to seeing Him all over the Bible. And looking back to your life before you formally met Him, like the two people on the road, you realise He was walking with you but you hadn't recognised Him yet.

When I was watching the TV series *Lost* as a teenager, I had no idea how lost I was. But I started to find myself in God when I found His hidden stories about Jesus in the Bible. Searching for the bigger picture to see that Jesus was always there in your life shows you that you have always been cradled in His arms and why your past was the way it was.

When Rahab first got that scarlet cord, if I were to guess, it was a gift to her. She would have had no idea that it would be the symbol that not only saved her family, but also a symbol of salvation for thousands of years to come for all humanity. Gifts are to be received, not earned.

Have you received the gift of Jesus?

Chapter Eight

Getting hidden revelation from 'boring' verses

If you want to know what God is saying to you personally today, you read the Bible. Even though it was written for many people to read, that does not mean God is only speaking to you in a generic non-personal way.

The Bible books were written in such a way that there is so much detail, and so much depth, that ten individuals could read the same verse and each person receive something specific and personal, different from the next.

Bible verses have been interpreted differently over the years, sometimes with serious consequences. The point for us is that the verses can also have different applications in our life's. Therefore each of those ten people could discover something from the same verse that the next person did not.

But how can your Bible reading experience be specific and personal when you, and let's say ten others, are all reading the same words? The answer is this: It's personal to you because the Holy Spirit makes it personal to you. He can take you somewhere specific with it. Yes - every verse, chapter and book are saying a specific and contextualised thing to a certain audience at a certain time in history, communicating particular information. The Holy Spirit can inspire different destinations from the same verse, even though we are all reading the same thing.

Picture these ten people standing in one room, all facing a mirror. Each one of them sees a slightly different reflection in the mirror due to the position they're standing in physically, emotionally, mentally and spiritually. And so the Holy Spirit draws you into a slightly different position every so often, as we move and grow and experience new things in life. The Spirit moves you so you see God's word differently, having had these new experiences over time, you see a wider angle of truth in His word. And for this reason, we can say that the Bible was written for many, but it speaks to all, personally, especially to those who love Him.

'Boring' verses

I want to talk about *'boring'* Bible verses and how we can extract life from them, by studying and meditating on them. I say *'boring'* verses not because they are boring, but because they're overlooked or underrated, or not seen as verses that you could get anything significant out of.

Now there are at least two reasons why the 'boring verse' strategy is so important. 1: if you can learn how to do this from the so-called boring verses, you can do it from any verse. 2: what this does is give you dynamic kinds of revelation, different from those you might normally be used to, and I'm going to give you examples of this.

We're so blessed to have all this scripture and sometimes I feel like we're spoiled. This strategy is all about seeing rich dynamic detail everywhere. We have so many verses to choose from we can often become biased and go to the obvious ones that are interesting, but in doing so we miss much depth in others. I believe that revelation can be drawn from verses in the Bible that many people would tend to disqualify as having any real significance.

You might think you need to experience certain things in your life in order for your eyes to be opened to certain verses, and that's true to an extent. But I want to show you that it's possible to reel in life from the most obscure places in the Bible, regardless of whether or not they speak to your personal circumstances. If you can learn how to do this, it will be one of the most exciting Bible reading strategies you can learn.

Gaining this skill gives you the ability to not only see the life in all the underrated verses, but also help to reinvigorate famous Bible verses that have lost their vitality and immediacy because you've heard them so many times. Before we begin, it's best to get into the right frame of mind. If I skipped this part it might not work as well.

Let's first prepare our hearts

The first thing I want to remind you that's important here is to remember that **"All scripture is God-breathed" 2 Timothy 3:16 (NIV).** When you read the Bible, know that you are reading the words of God. Either words that He said or words that He inspired man to write, God is behind every word. So if you think there are lots of books and verses in the Bible which are boring, or irrelevant, remember that this has come from the creator of everything, the creator of you, and that there is relevance in all of it for your life today because He loves you.

I think where there is truth, there is life. So if we agree that God is the author of truth and He is behind every word in the Bible, then there is also life in every word, all of them. This means we just need to find a way to draw the life from them.

Now, this is a more advanced strategy. I'm not sure I could've done it with much success when I first started reading the Bible, or even several years in. I had little understanding of it when I started, sometimes I could find interesting things in verses, but to find something of interest in *any* verse would have been very difficult. So if you're new to the Bible don't be put off if this doesn't yet work for you - learn it now to develop the awareness that all scripture has power in it, no exceptions.

When we go through these verses, I want you to treat them like they are the last verse you'll ever get to read. Sometimes I think we need to *decide* to be impacted, and that's really on you. Make a decision to be impacted before doing this.

Some people may question me on this one. But if God said it, even if it's the kind of verse that just connects important verses together, even then, there will be something in it. It's God's word.

I'm not the first person to talk about the value of single verse study or meditation, but just to be clear, I'm talking about all kinds of verses in the Bible having significant truth in them, not just the famous ones.

How do you do this?

There are two ways in which I want to demonstrate this:

1. Non-contextualized single verse study:
   This is just reading a verse on its own without looking at the surrounding verses and drawing life from that verse only. Now it's true that a Bible verse never stands alone and it gets its life from the scripture that surrounds it. But there is still a powerful way that you can get revelation from a given verse without immediately getting any context.

2. Contextualized single verse study:
   In order to draw the life from the verse, you learn about what's going on around it by reading the previous passages, commentaries, looking at videos and so on. Do whatever you need to do to draw life from that individual verse.

Now, which of the two do you choose from? Well that depends on the verse. If you can get away with seeing significant truths in the verse without context, try that first, but if you can't see any kind of revelation in the verse, then work on the context. Just read as far back as you need to go to know what's going on (sometimes you might need to look at other chapters or books to understand a verse better).

I want to put slightly more emphasis on the first way however, non- contextualised single verse study. *'But doesn't that mean you could risk changing the meaning of the verse if you have no context?'*

Yes, you could, so if you are not capable of this with the verse you select, then go to the second option and explore the context of the verse instead. The reason I want to put a little more emphasis on the first way is that I want to train you in how to get revelation with minimal resources.

Here's the thing: I think there is just as much value in so-called boring verses because this strategy gives us better access into more dynamic revelation. Of course, John 3:16 is a famous verse and of course, it's worthy of study, almost to an endless degree. But what I love about a boring verse Bible study, is that if you can study any of these, you will start to see the dynamic kind of information I'm talking about. Remember that the point of this is to teach you how to draw life from all scripture and to show you that there is a world of dynamic revelation in the Bible that is less immediately obvious.

I have taken the time to explain all this first because you may be surprised by the examples in this chapter. Okay, enough preparation. Let's begin.

Example one, a 'boring' verse with no context - Deuteronomy

So here's what I want to do, I've chosen a selection of verses and I want to talk about each one. In this first verse, I want to go with the first method, which is with no context at all. So here is Deuteronomy 5:30 (NIV):

"Go, tell them to return to their tents."

That's it. What on earth could you possibly take from this? Bear with me.

I should point out that this strategy only really tends to work if you have a good level of experience of Bible reading already. If you have barely read the Bible and know little of who God is, then you will not have the same number of scriptural reference points as a more experienced reader might - you will have less knowledge to link this to a revelation.

So on to the verse. The main thing that stands out to me in my first reading of this verse is the word *'tents'*. Now because I've decided beforehand that I'm going to draw something from this verse - before I look at it - it's as though I've just locked myself in with the verse. I don't want to make stuff up, I don't want to over spiritualise anything. It might sound a little silly to begin with, but then, I start to see something. So again - here's the verse:

"Go, tell them to return to their tents."

We don't have a lot to work with here, but the word *'tents'* stands out a little. I started to think that God gave humans the ability to come up with inventions like tents - He gave us the creativity to do this.

This takes my thinking to the next point of contact.

In the very first verse in the Bible, God shows us one of his attributes. Genesis 1:1: **"In the beginning God created the heavens and the earth" (NASB).**

So I think to myself, the attribute of God that He used to kick start the whole plan of humanity was creativity. He gave this same attribute to us.

I've been inspired by this verse to take me down a route here, starting from the word *'tents'*. Where can we go now? You know the reason I've mentioned a couple of times; that the value of boring verse studies is in the dynamic information we can draw from them. We can end up becoming re-acquainted with truths that we've always taken for granted.

So what am I seeing in this verse? God is creative, He is also the only true originator. He didn't give humans the ability to be truly original, but He did let us into creativity.

You know any time you find a truth in the Bible that you're captivated by, one of the best ways to push that truth further into you is by meditating on it. It pushes the truth further in you, making it more likely to stay and affect you. You let that truth scan your thoughts. What depths are there to discover by meditating on how creative God is and how He shows this? There are deeper places we can go from here, and it only started with the word *'tents'*.

But hold on a second, some might be reading this and thinking I'm taking it too far, that I'm *reading into it* too much. I don't think I am. I know this verse in Deuteronomy 5:30 isn't talking about creation, but why shouldn't it inspire me to think about it?

And here's the thing, who meditates on the fact that God is a creator? I don't know anyone who does, because it's a truth that is taken for granted and then its importance dissipates. A truth like this can get lost among all the amazing information we have in the Bible. There's so much to be explored that we can miss.

Now I know this verse itself is not talking about us having an ability to be creative. But the point is that the Holy Spirit can bring you to remembrance of other verses, which can then take you further along the journey of more truth being revealed to you. Jesus said this shortly before going on the cross **"But the Helper, the Holy Spirit, whom the Father will send in My name, He will teach you all things, and bring to your remembrance all that I said to you"** John 14:26 (NASB)

So when we lock ourselves in with one 'boring' verse, having prior experience with a lot of other scripture, we are able to think of other, similar verses that can lead us into something.

You might say *'the word 'tents' is in Deuteronomy 5:30, but it's also in the dictionary! Couldn't I just look out the window, see any old object and meditate on that?!'*

Well, you could. If you look out the window and decide to meditate on the first thing you see, let's say a car, and spend 5 minutes meditating on this with some relation to God, then fair play to you. If you get some God honouring, perspective-changing biblical revelation through doing this somehow, then why not?

But my point is to show you how to get revelation from anywhere in the Bible, *within your Bible reading session* - as opposed to picking and choosing an object to meditate on. So the Bible becomes our hub to get us started and inspire these kinds of things, as reading scripture brings us a certain spiritual charge to begin the process.

If doing this can bring a person to a point where through their meditation on God being a creator, they achieve a deep level of revelation or discovery, then there is no issue here for me personally. But if you happened to go on holiday to a campsite and saw a group of tents, you're probably not going to be in a state where you're inspired to think about such things.

Another point I would like to make is that I don't believe any scriptures in the Bible are only applicable to one person or a group of people at a one-off time. When Paul was asking Timothy to bring his cloak and scrolls to him in prison in 2 Timothy 4:13, I don't think this verse was for Paul's benefit only. I think God has put all the verses in the Bible to serve us in one form or another. The Holy Spirit can inspire, and when you open yourself up to that, you waste nothing in scripture.

Do you see what we can take from this? Dynamic revelation! It may seem a little wild, I know that. You can go further with this verse by just meditating on the truth of God sharing His creativity with us. I have only just explained this up to the point where I feel the revelation can be explored, and that point would be to meditate on the fact that God is creative. We could go much further still. But I want to move on to the next verse to show you how much potential there is in these kinds of verses.

Do you see how powerful this is yet? Not quite?

Up until this point I have attempted to set the scene and demonstrate this strategy. Let me continue with my next example.

Example two, a 'boring' verse with context - Joshua

100% of the verses in the Bible are life-giving, partly because there is a spiritual blessing in all of God's words whether you understand them with your mind or not. There is always power in absorbing His word.

I believe there is specific power behind each verse in the Bible, but some of the time we're unlikely to understand the specific blessing in every single verse. Such as, those concerning people whose names are in a genealogy that we have no other reference or information about. Now do I believe there is specific significance in the lives of all these people we don't know about? Absolutely, but how likely is it that your average Bible reader is going to know about this information? Probably not likely at all. There is still life in all scripture from the spiritual blessing it brings us however, even if you don't understand it with your head.

So this time I'll give you another boring verse. With this one, I'm going to give you the context. Bear in mind I have specifically looked for verses here that a lot of people would consider to be not all that important. I want to show you that all scripture is highly valuable. So here is my second example Joshua 19:11:

"Going west it ran to Maralah, touched Dabbesheth, and extended to the ravine near Jokneam" Joshua 19:11 (NIV)

That's it! That's the verse. I'll give you some context, and then let's read it again to see where we can go with it.

So this verse is speaking of the time when the Israelites, God's chosen people, have entered the famous Promised Land that they have been longing to enter for ages. Wars have been fought, kings have been defeated, walls have fallen. And now God is giving each of the twelve tribes of Israel a portion of the Promised Land that they can live in.

This chapter and verse are describing the geographical borders that God is giving to Zebulun, one of the twelve tribes of Israel. This is the *on the ground* contextual way to interpret the verse, where there is only ONE interpretation, it means what it means. Simple enough. But if we read it again now that we are loaded up with some small context, it aids our ability to *apply it in various ways*.

So then we can see that the difference between interpretation and application is much like the difference between drinking water because our thirst needs to be satisfied, to drinking water because our thirst needs to be satisfied to enable us to undertake different kinds of activities.

"Going west it ran to Maralah, touched Dabbesheth, and extended to the ravine near Jokneam" Joshua 19:11 (NIV)

So it's talking about the land borders that God is giving this tribe. Now I get that not everyone is going to want to study or meditate on a verse like this. I think one of the main reasons people think like this, is because they think it's too far away from them, it's too detailed, too irrelevant, there's nothing in it for them, or maybe it would be interesting for specialists but not your average Bible reader. I can't dictate to you how far you should go, however I want to show you that it's there if you want it. I want to show you that it's not just for the experts and theologians.

Any time we read the Bible, there's life to be drawn from it that can be poured out onto others somehow. But I want to show you here that this kind of verse can be relevant for you also. How do we take something from this verse and apply it to our lives today?

Here's the trail of thought. Before we apply it to our life, we first apply it to Jesus' life in order to create a bridge for the meaning to reach us. We need Jesus as the linking tool that makes it life-giving and relevant to us.

So we draw a line from this verse to Jesus, in that Jesus is God, and therefore the earth and all the land, all these portions of land that this passage speaks of, are His. They belong to Jesus.

That's the quick way to draw a line from this verse in Joshua, to Jesus. The land was distributed to God's people, but the land belongs to God, He was just loaning it out to them. And because Jesus is God, it all belongs to Jesus. Now then, how do we draw a line from Jesus to us today?

Well, the first thing that came to mind when I meditated on this was a verse in Romans 8:17, where it says **"Now if we are children, then we are heirs—heirs of God and co-heirs with Christ" (NIV)**. Notice the word *'heirs'*. It's saying that we as believers are co-heirs with Christ. Okay, stop for a second here. Remember what I said earlier, we are studying boring verses to discover dynamic revelation from them. Here's one of them. We are co-heirs with Christ. Now, what does that mean? Because that sounds pretty big.

It means we are co-receivers with Jesus. This then led me to think of Hebrews 9:15 (NIV) **"those who are called may receive the promised eternal inheritance"**. Notice the words **'promised inheritance'** like the inheritance that was promised to the Israelites that they part received in this 'boring' verse, Joshua 19:11.

Following on from this, Hebrews 9 talks about how if you are in someone's will, you must prove the death of the one who died, because the will is only in force when the person dies.

So when Jesus died, that's when His will kicked in, enabling us as His followers to become His co-heirs and receive the inheritance. Do you see? That's amazing! It's like what happened centuries ago in the book of Joshua with the allotting of the land. We can now see this as a prophetic bigger picture of the work of the cross. Let me explain.

The Exodus generation of Israel had to die in the wilderness before the new one could take the inheritance, the Promised Land, as is spoken of in part in Joshua 19:11, our so-called 'boring' verse. This points forward to how Jesus had to die for us so we could receive our spiritual inheritance. Amazing.

Or to put it a different way, the death of the Exodus generation in the desert parallels the death of Jesus. When they died in the desert, it gave the green light for the new generation to move into the Promised Land (Joshua 1:1-2). When Jesus died on the cross centuries later, it gave the green light for believers to receive the promised Holy Spirit (John 16:7), and in a sense enter the Promised Land, heaven on earth.

Aside from this awesome revelation and seeing how this Joshua verse links to other places in the Bible, here's what we can get from it. It reminds us that we have an inheritance from God. This is what I am taking home from this boring verse. If you were told that you would one day inherit a huge mansion, how would you feel? You would probably feel excited right? If some time passed and you got a call one day that you would soon be able to move into this mansion, your excitement would be greater than it was before, it would feel closer, it would feel more real. And then some more time passes and you get the keys - your excitement hits the roof!

Now because I followed this trail of truth which started in Joshua 19:11, I am getting more excited about the inheritance that I am, by God's law, legally due. In Hebrews 1:2 it says Jesus has been **"appointed heir of all things" (NASB)** and we are co-heirs with Him.

Now here's the thing and this is important. I knew about us getting an inheritance before reading these verses, but sometimes you need to hear a truth from a different angle in order for it to 'click' - in order for you to be moved by it.

We see the truth of our inheritance played out physically in the verse from Joshua. This then makes this spiritual truth of being co-heirs with Christ more clear and real to us now. And it started from this so-called boring verse in Joshua 19:11 **"Going west it ran to Maralah, touched Dabbesheth, and extended to the ravine near Jokneam"**.

The Holy Spirit took me on a little journey of truth which began in this verse in Joshua. He reminded me of various other verses, to help me see the life in this verse. As soon as you can link a verse to Jesus, it can sprout into all sorts of branches that you can run with and take something from.

Recap

Let me recap the process of getting life from a verse like Joshua 19:11.

- First, you find a boring verse from flicking through the Bible. When you find one, develop the intention (decide) to go somewhere profound with it.

- Next, get some context for the verse. That might mean reading previous verses and skimming over some of the previous chapters. Do as much as you need to do to get a refresher and know what is going on.

- After this, now you have context, the next thing to do is to try and draw a line from the verse to Jesus. How could you link the verse to Him, what does the verse have in common with Jesus? That's when the Hebrews verses came to mind for me.

- Then try to draw a line from Jesus to us today through that verse, to make the verse mean something that is practical or functional for your life today. All Old Testament scripture has meaning for us today when we convert it through Jesus into our lives. Don't think the Old Testament is there to just teach us interesting things, it's there to empower us.

- Throughout this process, pray and meditate – ask for guidance from the Holy Spirit – and then other verses may come to mind that bring you to a revelation.

Why do this at all? Because if you can learn how to do this, it will unlock more of the Bible for you. This strategy – and all the others – gives you a greater capacity to find more revelation, and accumulated over time more revelation lights a match to reveal another aspect of Jesus for you to see.

I want to point out that I didn't commit all the scriptures I've referenced in this example to memory – I don't know them off by heart. I simply meditated on the verse in Joshua, and then I was reminded of other small sections of scripture (and I had to search on the internet for these in order to know where the verses actually came from).

The reason I am mentioning this is to show you that you don't need to know scripture so well (i.e. you don't need to memorise and quote verses all day long) to do this. But if you have some level of experience reading scripture, then when the Holy Spirit brings thoughts of passages into your mind, you can easily just search on the internet from there to find the actual verse number.

I acknowledge that this revelation I received may or may not excite anyone. It was exciting to me because it was revealed to me. More importantly, I want to show you the principle that this can be done. When you understand that revelation is not always so far away, you then have an incredible strategy to see things you didn't before.

Example three, a 'boring' verse with no context again

In this last example, here is another verse for us to read with no context, like the first example.

"After these things, Jesus was walking in Galilee" John 7:1 (NASB)

My first thought was the word 'walking' - there's not much else to work with if we don't have any context. And so the thought is of Jesus walking. I think each of the verses I'm talking about in this chapter should be approached in different ways, so after

Getting hidden revelation from 'boring' verses

looking at this verse and considering where it could take us, I felt that it would be best approached through meditation.

In the first example of this chapter I ended the section early instead of explaining the meditation element, so in this example that is where I will begin. So I got down on my knees, put my forehead to the ground, closed my eyes and meditated ('saw' in my mind's eye) on Jesus walking.

While on my knees, straight away I had a picture in my mind of an area that could be described as somewhere in Israel, sunny, dry, rural, only a few people around, and this particular area was fairly flat. I was standing up, and straight away I saw Jesus through a heat haze. It was the first time I've ever seen Him. He was dressed in a white, or maybe an off-white robe. And He was walking. Not walking directly towards me, but walking towards my left, so I had to slowly track my eyes left to stay on Him. There were a couple of people with Him, He was slightly in front of them, maybe just a metre ahead.

My first reaction was that I was stunned, quickly breathing in through my mouth, a gasp that could be heard. There was so much going on in my mind, but the first thought that I had, that stood out in front of my other thoughts, and that I could make any sense of, was that He was walking. It's strange sometimes, the things we observe first. I've seen people walking my whole life. But when I consider why this was my first thought, I think it was because it was God whom I could see walking. Yes, I know that God became man, of course. Yes, I know He had a human body, I have thought about this many times. But, now I was looking at the reality of this. I was still overwhelmed and emotionally disorientated, but there was something about watching Him walk that utterly captivated me.

If you were to ask me what I would say to Jesus if I had an hour with Him in person, I might speak of asking Him about what heaven is like. I might ask Him questions about reaching the lost. But now that I was actually looking at Him, all I wanted to do was just watch Him, I didn't want to ruin this moment. Just watching Him was beyond any satisfaction I could have dreamed of. I don't even feel I can do anything other than watch Him, because I feel a sense of paralysis.

And now my next thought rises from the emotional disorientation. I'm thinking to myself, should I be crying here? I feel that I should be, and that I almost want to be, there may be some more moisture over my eyes, but not enough to cry. And I realise why I cannot yet cry. I think back to times where I have cried, and it seems to happen after I have realised something. Crying is something that often comes after comprehending something, not during. There's too much going on to cry just now.

But then the next thought rises in my mind. And actually, I realise that this thought has been there from the moment I first saw Jesus, but it's only now that I am able to comprehend it. I think being emotionally disorientated means that we have so many thoughts and emotions going on that it takes time for us to make sense of any of them. And so I realise that this one was there from the start.

It is from John, writing in the book of Revelation. In Revelation 1, the apostle whom Jesus loved (John) sees Him in a vision. John was with Jesus for around three and a half years when Jesus came to earth, and this scene in the book of Revelation is approximately sixty years later. John has lived these sixty-something years having Jesus on his mind all the time. Living for Jesus every day. And now, after all these years, he sees Him again, two old friends reunited. But why do I think of this scene? It's because of what it says in verse 17:

"When I saw Him, I fell at His feet like a dead man. And He placed His right hand on me" Revelation 1:17 (NASB)

Now I understand. I understand why John fell at His feet like a dead man. I wondered about this verse for years, but now that I have meditated on seeing Jesus walking in front of me, I understand why John would react in such a way. And I understand why the perfect touch of Jesus' right hand was necessary to 'ground' John, detaching him from his overwhelmed state.

Then I stopped meditating. I can only hope you see the power of doing something like this. I have tried to explain this strategy as best as I can, strategy is perhaps not the strongest word for it however. It is so powerful.

Try it yourself

I understand that by reading the 'boring' verses I have chosen and hearing me talk about them you might not experience the revelation that I'm getting (maybe you would if you tried doing it with the same verses). You're just reading what I'm saying and it might not be personal to you. To feel this, you have to do it yourself. I'm just giving examples to give you a start if you're interested. Of course, that goes for all the strategies in this book.

I know when you read books it can be easy to skip over the exercises the author gives you. But can I suggest that you try this one now? Meditate on this verse I have selected from the book of Jude.

If you are in a quiet and calm environment, perhaps get on your knees, close your eyes and spend a few minutes experiencing any truth you can find in this verse. But just to reiterate what I said earlier, if you do this with other verses, do it in either one of two ways. Get no background or context for the verse and search for the truth in it this way. Or, if you feel that you cannot do that with the verse you've chosen (which could be at random) then get some context.

In this example I suggest you search out a revelation without any context. Lock yourself into this verse only, see if the Holy Spirit can take you somewhere:

"Jude, a servant of Jesus Christ and a brother of James, to those who have been called, who are loved in God the Father and kept for Jesus Christ" Jude 1:1 (NIV)

This can be done from so many places in scripture, probably every page. But the whole point is to show you that revelation is not that far away when your heart is prepared for it. Go in with that attitude - just decide you're going to get revelation.

I acknowledge many people will find this to be the most unusual chapter in this book. And I acknowledge that many Christians will struggle to use this strategy if they're not ready for it. I have even been laughed at for this one! But I am adamant that I should include it. As I have written much of this chapter I have felt that the content might split the readership. Some may not be able to connect with these ideas, whiles others can. Personally for me, it's one of the most exciting and unexplored strategies in this book, but will be almost useless unless you stop and truly consider the verses. Do I expect anyone to do single verse Bible studies every day? Not really, but it's a powerful strategy to have at hand whenever you want it.

Revelation is available on every page of the Bible, with zero exceptions. What determines the ones you see and the ones you don't see? I would say it's got something to do with the life you are living and your experiences, which can somehow trigger revelation when you read the Bible. I do think one of the most powerful things you can do to unlock revelation is by living a life for God, by actually walking with Him daily. Doing things for Him, expanding your comfort zone, living a life of faith, and reading scripture alongside this.

Progressively living a life of faith more and more as you get older will reveal more truths in the Bible, fuelling your desire to live for Him still more. If Christians do none of this and continue to never truly grow, reading the scriptures will feel flat and lifeless because they don't relate to what they say.

It's like carrying the calf from one village to the next, every single day, expecting to get stronger and stronger until you can carry it as a bull. God has designed life in such a way where if we live life and do things the same way all the time, we will hit plateaus and stop growing and getting stronger, like the man who tried to carry a bull. We must put ourselves in a position to grow and be open to the unexpected.

Waking up to the reality that the words in the Bible are true. Waking up to the reality that Jesus did die on the cross for us. Waking up to the reality that all the things the Bible talks about that are happening. A child wonders in awe that God created the heavens and the earth, but an adult forgets how amazing that is.

In the first example in this chapter I talked about meditating on the fact that God is creative. Who meditates on the fact that Jesus has a pair of legs and walks? People don't tend to meditate on these kinds of things. But when you do this, you start to realise that there are so many amazing hidden places in scripture that you can meditate on. Verses like this are the kind of hidden linking verses that people don't consider as having that much importance. But that's why they give dynamic kinds of revelation because they're overlooked and taken for granted.

At the very start of the book of Hebrews, it says **"In the past God spoke to our ancestors through the prophets at many times and in various ways, but in these last days he has spoken to us by his Son" Hebrews 1:1-2 (NIV)**

This means if you want to hear from God, you read the Bible - because it is all about the Son. Jesus breathes over every single verse. And it's personal, even though it was written for many. It's still personal to you because the Holy Spirit makes it so, and He can take you where you need to go with it.

If you struggle to hear God regularly, it is not because He has nothing to say to you, He is *walking* with you. He can speak to you personally through the Bible. Don't be afraid to let the Holy Spirit take you on a journey. Don't be afraid of being accused of *reading into the verse* and experimenting with scripture.

And if you suspect you are going too far, bring it to your pastors to get their opinion and refine your ability to hear from Him. Learn how to be spiritually intuitive, learn how to be aware of what He says.

I have given some examples of what it can be like to study these verses that are really not boring at all. And for me, it was electrifying to find these truths. But I don't expect you to feel much from my revelation, I just want to show you that this is indeed a thing you can do. Use this tool however you like. If you learn this, you can use it for any verse you feel the need to spend time on. If you can gain this skill you will be able to learn some of the deepest insights into God that He has made available to us.

Chapter Nine
Viewing life through scripture

Jesus replied, "But even more blessed are all who hear the word of God and put it into practice." Luke 11:28 (NLT)

Some say that the greatest skill that you can learn is the skill of learning how to gain a skill. One of the greatest skills a Christian can learn is the skill of being able to apply God's word in their life. How do you do this? How do you put God's word in you, so that it becomes you?

Luke chapter 9 talks about the cost of following Jesus. It shows us three short conversations that Jesus had with three different people, all about following Him. What Jesus said to each of these people forced them to rethink whether or not they really wanted to follow Him. Jesus tested their attitudes so they could be aware of what they *really* believed.

It might be that at a certain point in your journey, if you

read and study these verses in Luke 9, you won't be able to do anything other than question your own life and the way you do things. These verses have caused many Christians to look at their lives and question if they have really submitted themselves to God as much as they think they have.

As they were going along the road, someone said to Him, "I will follow You wherever You go." And Jesus said to him, "The foxes have holes and the birds of the air have nests, but the Son of Man has nowhere to lay His head."

And He said to another, "Follow Me." But he said, "Lord, permit me first to go and bury my father." But He said to him, "Allow the dead to bury their own dead; but as for you, go and proclaim everywhere the kingdom of God."

Another also said, "I will follow You, Lord; but first permit me to say goodbye to those at home." But Jesus said to him, "No one, after putting his hand to the plough and looking back, is fit for the kingdom of God." Luke 9:57-62 (NASB)

When the time comes for us to apply the word, we see what we really believe. Do we believe God's word? Do we want to live it? Are we really willing to permit Jesus into our life this way? How can we even handle such a thing, when Jesus wants our everything?

Let the word search out your life

If you want to explore a Bible passage that has a particularly significant and current meaning to you, one of the greatest ways that you can get to know it really well is by living with it so you can start to see the world *through* it. This is the skill of *applying the word.*

Load yourself up with a particular biblical truth that you believe God is calling you to grasp right now by meditating on it each and every day. Keep it in your life for long enough to give it the opportunity to seek out and speak into your everyday blind spots. You are letting the passage search out things in your life so that it can shine a light on things you have overlooked.

It doesn't work as well when you try to meditate on the passage in your Bible reading session only, because you are not giving the verses the *opportunity* to seek out things in your day to day life. The beauty of this is that you give more permission to God to decide what to speak into, rather than you deciding, because He will call your mind to the truth of the passage at the most necessary moments each day.

I'm not saying you need to try as often as you can throughout the day to remind yourself at a conscious level of the passage currently on your heart. But if you are doing things like a) spending time meditating on it, reading and re-reading it, b) looking for similar scriptures, c) looking at commentaries, d) speaking to other Christians about the passage, d) seeking even deeper and broader understanding, e) praying and asking God questions about it, you give the scripture, or rather the Holy Spirit, the opportunity to remind you of it at the very time it is needed in your day, rather than you trying to remember it.

If there is a particular truth in the Bible that resonates with you, more so than is usual, then find a way to get it into you every day. In this way it becomes a part of your thinking, giving you deeper insight into how you might go about living out this truth in your life. This will help you to turn the passage into a revelation and something that's part of your character and behaviour.

Sometimes what's required for you to *get* a passage, for the revelation to click, to reel it in closer, is to bring it with you every day. Take it to work. Take it with you on your way home. Keep it with you while watching TV. Seeking God's voice on a passage, over days or even weeks, will mean it is never too far from the front of your mind and you won't have to try and remember it, because recall will just happen automatically from your contemplation.

So if you were to live with these verses in Luke 9 for example, you might think to yourself, *"what is it I need to let go? What area of my life have I not given to Him?"* These are questions you may find difficult to answer right away - on the spot - so you need to view things in your everyday life, hour by hour, thought by thought, as they happen, *through* the scriptures that are impacting you.

With the number of different thoughts we have every day, loading yourself up with certain scriptures will enable you to screen your thoughts with the biblical truth that is in your heart, giving that particular truth better leverage to work into you and change you.

Kingdom culture

People have always, whether they are Christian or not, viewed the world from a certain perspective. You have a particular perspective on life whether or not you are even aware of it. Viewing the world through a certain set of paradigms that have been set by someone else and that continue through people is a component of human culture. Every family has their own culture, every group of friends, every workplace, every town, city and nation. They all have a culture that tends to be determined by the most dominant perspective, which starts with the imposition of a set of beliefs about things. And from there, that particular setting starts to influence the way we feel. This often informs the attitudes of people in any given staff room, in any given office, in any given organisation.

We see in the book of Daniel that Daniel viewed things in the world in a certain way. He was exiled from his nation and taken captive by another, a nation that also viewed the world in a certain way. But because Daniel's view of the world was from the heart of God, and because Daniel continued to live in God's culture despite being in a new one, he imbued the new place he was in with kingdom culture. Daniel, being aware of who God was, let God into a situation where it might have been tempting to turn a blind eye to Him. It is clear that Daniel viewed things in life through God's truth because he took God with him, he didn't leave Him in the back of his mind in everyday situations, he didn't deny Jesus like Peter did when the emotions got tense.

God has the absolute view on all things, and therefore He can perfectly inform us on how we should view things. So when we view certain things from His heart, we strike a match in an area that was not lit before. Sin has utterly corrupted our world and darkened it, and so the only way that we can see any truth in it is from the vantage point of His heart.

If you are a Christian working in a secular workplace, you can change the culture there by letting God's power in. No matter how long-established that culture is, God can work His way in, through you, when you walk with Him. If you can't, then perhaps God will take you out of that culture, as He did with Lot in Sodom and Gomorrah (Genesis 18 and 19).

When we are captivated by a particular truth in the Bible, we work that truth into our lives by viewing the world through it. And to view the world through it, you need to load yourself up with it by regular meditation on that truth, in order to affect the culture of your mind and heart. This means it will naturally come out of you without a conscious effort to remember it, and it will thus affect the physical culture around you, like Daniel.

The progressive journey of faith

The scriptures become more real when we experience the things they talk about. We experience them by applying them, and we apply them by living with and meditating on them till they become a part of the way we think. We give them leverage into our lives.

To let God into the areas we know we need Him is one thing, but to give Him access into the areas where we don't know we need Him, is another. So the scriptures can root out all the hidden areas of your life when you meditate on the truths God has brought to your attention. It becomes less about you deciding where you need God and more about Him deciding.

Often when people asked Jesus questions, He would give them indirect answers, not answering their questions from the front, but answering them so that restoration might come to the root of the issue. He understood the issue so well that He could do this instantly. But when He taught people this way, you can't help but think that the individuals were disappointed by His response, because they wanted a quick fix. Instead, He gives the cure.

His teachings are to be applied into our lives by the vehicle of faith. We apply these apparently *'hard'* teachings by faith. We hold on to the sins in our lives, like bad attitudes, addictions, or pride, because losing them would be like death to us on the inside. But the restoration of life in these areas becomes possible by faith alone - by God's power, not yours. So when people were disappointed by Jesus's responses, they were disappointed because they contemplated the thought of doing what He said in their own strength, rather than by faith, which they didn't yet seem to understand. When you do things by faith you are empowered by Him, because with faith there is always an exchange.

In Luke 12:13-21, we have the parable of the rich fool. Someone called out to Jesus and asked Him to order his brother to give him his fair share of his family inheritance. But instead of Jesus involving Himself in the matter, a type of problem He did not come to earth for, Jesus instead told him to beware of greed and how life is not measured by what you own. Jesus then gave a parable, teaching the kingdom perspective on wealth, teaching a perspective that would solve this man's issues from the heart. This man wanted Jesus's help for his issue from a superficial angle - but Jesus knew what he really needed.

So if God has asked, or ever does ask you to do something that might seem impossible for you, whether it is to do a certain thing or give something up, consider that He might not be expecting you to solve things straight away. But what He does want is for you to be led by Him step by step in a way that eventually progresses you to be able to do that thing you thought was impossible.

Recognise that walking in faith to achieve the impossible is often a progressive journey that starts with doing many smaller things that are possible for you. Don't be intimidated by the size of the mountain. Individual steps are easier to take. But you are letting God decide what those steps are, rather than being overwhelmed by trying to decide what they are yourself and being disappointed - like the man in the parable of the rich fool.

One of the biggest deceptions we can face as Christians is letting God into the obvious areas, such as our pains, our heartbreaks, our obvious emotional needs and desires, but not letting Him into the areas that cause these things in the first place. Often we don't even know what these are. They are our blind spots as Christians.

We live with and meditate on the scriptures in order for them to become a part of our natural daily thoughts. This gives them the power to root out the blind spots. If you think you can't stop having lustful thoughts or watching porn, or you can't forgive someone that has brought harm to you, have you considered that you have tried to give God the right thing but in the wrong order? The answer might be that it's not about trying your hardest not to have those thoughts, or not to go on those websites, or to pretend you love the person who wronged you.

Have you considered that if you don't give Him your time by reading the Bible every day and seeing the world through His word, you won't be able to give Him these self-proclaimed impossibilities? When you live life by faith, God takes you on a progressive journey to do the 'impossible', to move mountains, to move bulls, but in the order He shows you, not the order you show yourself.

When you train yourself to view the world through a Bible passage that resonates with you, you give it the opportunity to find a route into your life that might not be the one you expected. You give God the opportunity to teach you something on His terms.

Sometimes God will ask you to do a big thing, a thing that seems impossible. But faith can take you on a progressive journey that brings you to the point where you can do that impossible thing.

Experiencing the word

Grace is a fascinating subject. A person becomes a Christian, and the penny drops about what grace is. But soon after, they mess up morally, skip church on Sunday, go in the next week, but still feel broken and ashamed. Then someone in church reminds them that the guilt they feel is not from God, and in fact, God still wants to bless them. This revives them emotionally and they gain their strength back, more so than before.

The greater experience of grace however, is when it empowers you so much, that you don't go back to the moral failure, so you don't need that emotional revival in the first place. And beyond that still, you become a person who is graceful to others, who blesses and loves others whether they deserve it or not. You go from being a grace 'academic' (someone who knows about it without direct experience) to someone who lives within grace, inside and out. And you see that grace is not *'unmerited favour'* and nothing else, but it also contains the power to want to please God because of gratitude for what Jesus did.

Therefore, we do not want to take advantage of the gift of grace, and we see that, in keeping God's ways, we experience a greater depth of His grace. We see that grace is to be understood, yes, but beyond that, it is to be experienced. And experiencing starts by letting the scriptures search your life.

"But prove yourselves doers of the word, and not merely hearers who delude themselves. For if anyone is a hearer of the word and not a doer, he is like a man who looks at his natural face in a mirror; for once he has looked at himself and gone away, he has immediately forgotten what kind of person he was." James 1:22-24 (NASB)

How do you live your life from the heart of God? You love people the way Jesus loves people, whether you feel like it or not, and this starts to reposition your heart so that it's in the same place as God's.

We want to get the word in us so that the Holy Spirit can remind us of it when He needs to. We all have a certain culture in our own minds, but then we add scripture so it changes to that of kingdom culture. It just works so much better when we ingest scripture at the deepest level. Then it starts to work through us without us having to try so hard, without us striving to be better Christians.

There really is a difference between knowing the word and experiencing it. If you have ever led someone to God, many scriptures will stand out to you more because of this. If you have seen miracles, you will see more of them in the Bible, because of this. If your prayer life is becoming more powerful, you will see this kind of thing in the scriptures more than you did before, because of this. If you are starting to carry the bull, the impossibilities made possible that you read of in the Bible will stand out to you more, because of this.

The scriptures will become more powerful. As a result, you will see the power you couldn't have before. When you absorb a passage in the Bible, you start to see the world through those words, you start to see through that layer in your everyday life, even as you walk down the street.

So after all this, how do you know what scripture to meditate on? The quick answer is that you will know when you need to. Have you ever read certain Bible verses and then the pastor happens to be preaching on those same verses around that time? It's funny how often that happens. Sometimes this is an indication that we need to camp out on those verses. That's an example of how it *could* happen.

But really, it just starts when you read a particular passage and you know in your heart that you need to get that truth and live it out. God has designed us this way, He convicts us with things that we need to get. If you are interested to know how this works for some of us, let me attempt to explain.

The process by which scripture changes us

When you meditate on a certain scripture enough, as I've said previously, the truth from this scripture will start to outwork itself from you and become real and practical in your life. But before this happens, *you* outwork yourself into the scripture. Let me explain.

Preceding the moment when you are captivated by a certain truth in the Bible, when you come across verses that are so meaningful to you (verses that you know you need to spend time on) something was happening in your life relating to the verses. This means that when you read them, you were primed and prepared to be captivated by them because of something that was going on in your life, an event, circumstance or thought pattern.

God has brought about a theme through thoughts or certain circumstances in your life that has been going on for a period of time. Then at some point either planned or unplanned, you read verses that relate to this theme of thinking. The verses captivate and have a profound effect on you, and this is the time when you meditate on them, keeping them in your life to absorb and explore them. If you have done this for a long enough time, they start to come back out of you and you start to view things in life through them.

But this time, the theme you originally had is now more informed than it was before when it first came to you. The scripture that captivated you has prepared your initial thoughts to be better understood, detailed, purposed and empowered by God. The prophet Isaiah talks about this:

"The rain and snow come down from the heavens and stay on the ground to water the earth. They cause the grain to grow, producing seed for the farmer and bread for the hungry. It is the same with my word. I send it out, and it always produces fruit. It will accomplish all I want it to, and it will prosper everywhere I send it." Isaiah 55:10-11 (NLT)

Isaiah talks about how God's word goes on a journey to reach us and then comes back out of us. As you continue to see the world through the verses and keep going back to them, you begin to see even more in them than before, because you are now living with them. It's the beautiful life cycle of God's word.

God speaks to us in our everyday lives in many different ways. This shapes and conditions our thinking on a specific subject, one that we are perhaps not yet clear on or even conscious of, but it becomes something we need. We read the Bible and at just the right time, a certain passage screams out to us because it resonates with the subject that has been on our minds. So, as we seek clarity, we read the passages, and re-read them, each day, meditating, seeking, praying and exploring them even further so we begin to see the world *through* the passage. We receive revelation at just the right time, and now, this subject that was amongst our thoughts and life circumstances for a while, comes back out of us, but more organised, more informed, more understood and dressed in the robes of Jesus, tasked with an objective from His will.

The greatest revelation of all

The greatest reality to be aware of is the reality that Jesus became flesh, died for our sins and rose again. However, I am not convinced that anyone other than Jesus could live by this reality fully and unhindered. As sinners, we are partially blinded and therefore simply cannot do this with total clarity, but when we have a continual refreshing of the same revelation that the Bible constantly presents – but from different angles - it further enhances our ability to live closer to this reality.

All biblical revelations you have, no matter what they are about, have built inside of them an arrow that convicts you more of the work of Jesus on the cross. Furthermore, your revelation or unveiling of truths that were previously unknown to you, as powerful as they may be on their own, are merely slide shows to the main feature, the spiritual drive to live your life for Jesus. This is what all revelation brings to us.

When you do things for God, if you say you are doing them for Him and not for yourself, that is a noble and humble thing. But what is greater still than this, is when you do things for God not as an obedient servant who knows nothing of the heart of your master, but because your heart has become the same as your master's. This is our greatest revelation.

Do you know what the final stage of learning a skill is?

Learning a skill is based on learning something so thoroughly that the way you test out what you have learned is by moving on from it and letting go. So the last phase of learning a skill is forgetting it in order to become it. Therefore, we let the scriptures dissolve and disappear into our stomachs when we close our Bibles, like sweet honey. They go into our veins, into our character, coming back out of us like light, like the glowing shepherd boy, who was searching for God's own heart. It is only when we let go of the word, when we finish our Bible reading session for the day, that we can see what has become of it, and what we have become.

'The Lord has sought out for Himself a man after His own heart' 1 Samuel 13:14 (NASB)

The most significant thing that David did to show that he was searching for God's own heart, and indeed lived from it, was his demonstration of utter closeness to God through his psalms.

Actually no. Not closeness, but oneness.

Closeness is almost there, but oneness is in the middle of God's eye. David felt what God felt. A man that searched for God's own heart so that he could be in God's heart. When he wrote psalms, David would often write in line with God's perspective, as if using tracing paper over God's thoughts so that they became his own - to such an extent that those very words would one day be fit for King Jesus to say for Himself, repurposed for a greater meaning:

"Yet you brought me safely from my mother's womb and led me to trust you at my mother's breast. I was thrust into your arms at my birth. You have been my God from the moment I was born." (NLT)

David writes Psalm 22, so at one with God that we can also read this from the perspective of Jesus Himself, who uses the same words to describe His exact beginnings.

"My God, my God, why have You forsaken me?" (NASB) David writes Psalm 22, so at one with God, that we can also read this from the perspective of Jesus Himself, who says the same words when hanging on the cross.

"For you will not leave my soul among the dead or allow your holy one to rot in the grave." (NLT) David writes Psalm 16, so at one with God that we can also read this from the perspective of Jesus Himself, who uses the same words to describe His Resurrection.

The beautiful examples we have in scripture from David show that even though he was a sinner, it is possible to live from the heart of God by thinking, feeling, living and acting in the same way that God Himself would. Therefore, my friends, we need not experience God from a distance. As He is in us, so we are in Him, living, from the heart of God.

"But we all, with unveiled faces, looking as in a mirror at the glory of the Lord, are being transformed into the same image from glory to glory, just as from the Lord, the Spirit." 2 Corinthians 3:18 (NASB)

from glory to glory. Amen.

Acknowledgements

Allan Meredith for leading me to Jesus, thank you for giving me your time when I was seeking answers in life. **Edd McCracken** for general advice on the back end of writing a book. **George Alexander** for checking my theology and helping me to better understand God in my earlier days. **James Donaldson** for inspiring one of the boring Bible verses I selected, turns out it was cohesive with the rest of the book. **James Trower** for your friendship, guidance and for sparking the idea that led to this book, in general, thank you for everything. **Janet de Vigne** for editing the whole book and challenging many of my points. **Kitti Klempa** for giving me a non-Christian perspective on my book, I pray you meet the Lord soon. **Peter Anderson** for enabling the confidence I needed to write about certain theological points. **Paul James-Griffiths** for checking the theology in my book and being an inspiration to me. **Steph Sharkey** for reading over my book and giving valuable feedback and support. **Shaun Cumming** for giving me another non-Christian perspective and being a lifelong friend. **Tzephanyahu** for giving me insights on difficult parts of scripture like no other.

Thank you all so much, without you I would not have had this dream come true.